GATHER

Together Women Change the World

Christy Dreiling

Gather Publishing
ASHLAND, OREGON

Christy Dreiling/Gather Publishing
www.christydreiling.com

Editing by Susan Strecker and Stephanie Gunning
Book Production by Stephanie Gunning Enterprises
Cover design by Gus Yoo
Book Layout © Book Design Templates

Ordering Information: Special discounts are available on quantity purchases by corporations, associations, and others. For details, contact the publisher at the website above.

Library of Congress Control Number: 2019933479

Gather/Christy Dreiling —1st edition
978-0-578-48128-9 (paper)

Contents

To Sage, my first grandbabe

"Each time a woman stands up for herself, without knowing it possibly, without claiming it, she stands up for all women."

–MAYA ANGELOU

AUTHOR'S NOTE

I ENCOURAGE YOU TO LOOK for a Gather Group in your area. If there is not one, text, email, or phone a few friends with whom you want to grow and take this journey together. There are eleven chapters full of suggestions for topics to discuss.

INTRODUCTION

IT IS TRULY SURPRISING THAT I ever began
to work with women because as a younger woman I
never really liked being with other women much.
Back then, I preferred hanging with the guys—my
boyfriend at any given time and his male friends,
and later on, my husband. Although it's ironic,
given my preference for male friends, that I built a
multimillion-dollar sales team for a company that
mainly serves women, I sincerely love women today.
I have healed the rift with them that was a
consequence of mistrust born out of some negative
experiences I had in high school and adulthood.

I suppose the universe puts us right where we
are supposed to be to heal what's been missing. I
grew up with three sisters, nonetheless for too long

I would get anxiety just thinking of going to an event attended mostly by women. Just a few years ago I was at an executive leadership retreat where 90 percent of all the executives were women. You wouldn't find me downstairs where the party was, however; I was upstairs at the bar with the scientists and technologists who, in this case, all happened to be guys. Their company was where I felt most comfortable. Why was this? Deep down I wanted to be with the women, having fun. But I just couldn't let down my guard. It was too hard for me to let myself relax around them.

Let me assure you, it wasn't them. None of the women had been unwelcoming. It was my past experiences as a girl that led me to this insecurity. I needed to remove a block.

That's why I'm here, writing vulnerably and honestly, to share my heart with all women who also have struggled (or still struggle) and felt the same pain, whether a little or a lot, of not loving women's company or not feeling they safely can let loose and be their free-spirited selves around the women they know. We women have a bad reputation for being mean to one another and viciously competitive. This behavior has to stop. A change is overdue.

The choice to be supportive of one another's dreams and aspirations must start with us.

Amazing women have always surrounded me, and I have always wanted relationships with them, even when I was too afraid to open up. But this only became possible for me when I decided that I didn't want to live my entire life keeping a distance from those women. At first the thought of opening my heart was scary, but I took the risk and did it and it has been one of the best journeys I've ever taken. I treasure the friendships I've formed. The sisterhood of women in my business and my community makes me stronger.

Maybe you are one of the fortunate ones who has always felt secure in her skin or has never felt the pain of walking into a room that goes awkwardly silent because someone is talking about you behind your back. I have and it left me with a sense of dread. Maybe you've never been betrayed by a woman you shared your soul with, but too many of us have had friends gossip about us. Being compared to other females and comparing ourselves to airbrushed images in magazines can leave us feeling less than or not good enough.

Have you ever felt this way? It's tragic how many women do.

Some the most beautiful moments in my life have been with women and some of my saddest, too. There have been occasions when I felt ashamed for shining my light because it was obvious that my success made the women in my life uncomfortable. Instead of supporting me, they denigrated me. I spent a lot of years playing small because I didn't want to face the pain of standing out and needing to deal with the gossip, daggered looks, or insecurity of my peers.

Have you ever played down your abilities or denied your dreams to make others feel better about themselves when you were around? It doesn't feel good, does it? Many women I've talked to have cried wishing for unity and admitted they are concerned for their school-aged daughters. With social media, attacks from girl to girl or woman to woman can be meaner than they were just twenty years ago. What I hunger for and what these women hunger for is to belong to a community of women in which they can feel safe, loved, honored, and respected while being encouraged to dream and build.

Research states that 52 percent of fifteen-year-old girls show indirect aggression to their female counterparts versus 20 percent of boys of the same age. These findings are not shocking, but they do bother me. They have awakened me to the fact that our young women need female mentors to show them, guide them, and teach them that they are not alone. More than ever before, I strongly believe we need to band together rather than cut each other down. If we step forward as a group and take responsibility for the female role in this social misfortune, then maybe, just maybe, we can create change that will forever improve the lives of women everywhere around the world.

The purpose of this book is to awaken my fellow sisters of every age, race, culture, religion, and belief system. I believe if we want the world to change, as Gandhi is oft-cited as saying, "We must be the change we wish to see in the world." I imagine a world where are daughters, sisters, mothers, and friends no longer fear being themselves. I imagine a world where it's safe to be us no matter how unique, quirky, eccentric, and interesting we are.

It is my sincere belief that we are all artists in our own ways. We have come here to this beautiful planet to share our beauty. Not to be frightened by it or afraid of the light in others. We are the creators of our world and the creators of the world. I invite you to take a journey with me. Let's explore the inner depths of our souls. Let's work on it together, let's heal and love. Only then can we experience truly what it means to be women.

Before you dig any further, I ask that for change to happen we must gather our sisters, mothers, daughters, and friends. Let's create supportive discussion groups. Let's become each other's champions. I see girls and women of all ages starting their Gather Groups in their hometowns. I see us joining our hearts across the globe, over land and oceans.

1 WHY WE NEED OUR SISTERS

A WOMAN IS A DIVINE, beautiful, delicate, and complicated piece of art. For years our society has made fun of women's hormonal ups, downs, and sideways personalities. Actually, who are we kidding? We've all shared a few jokes about female mood swings. One day we're feeling on top of the world, the next we're weeping for no reason. We're happy, then mad. We're sad, then glad. We're alternately excited, freaked, entertaining, and indecisive. We're inventors, lovers, and artists. We're delicate. But we're also tough as hell.

We are women. We are the colors of life. We give birth, we feel, we love, we hurt, we screw up, and we get it right.

Here's the thing. Women and girls are not always kind to one another. Growing up, I was a girl who never hung around with other girls. Sometimes I found them mean. I didn't like them as much as boys. The truth is that I didn't even like myself much. Honestly, I'm still learning to like myself. But I do like and admire women now! And I want to help every woman and girl learn to love herself—or love herself more. I think this is something that can be reinforced by practicing showing one another love and respect.

And why should we expend energy lifting one another up? Because if the world is a tough place for us to live, we have a very real incentive to change it. Together we can change the world. One girl or woman can't do it, *but lots* of girls and women can.

What no longer serves us must be changed. And we cannot depend on others to do it for us. We must initiate the change. Change may not have started with you and me, but we can take over from those who came before. We can collectively grab the helm of our lives and change the course our ship is steering. Change has to start with us. And it must begin now. Novice and wise women must come together to drive this beautiful ship of womanhood to a place called Change.

It won't be easy, but it is possible for women and girls to love themselves and each other. We have to roll up our sleeves and have passionate, loving, and open discussions about why we think and behave otherwise. Heck, I haven't even come close to having the answers yet, but I believe together we are better and stronger so we should begin trying to figure it out. We can figure this out together and become one.

I believe each of us needs to start doing some *heartwork*. Your "heart" is the real you. Your head does a lot of talking but sometimes (actually most of the time) it lies. The head might tell us we should be afraid, that we're not good enough, or that people are criticizing us behind our backs and cannot be trusted. If what goes on in our heads were adapted for TV, it'd be a top drama on Netflix. The big fat stories the head makes up aren't real, and yet we get totally worked up over them. Once we can accept that the heart is a wiser guidance system, we will begin to experience more effortless relationships and have more fun leading the great big, gorgeous lives we all get to live!

My research for this book has revealed that, in part, women are competitive with one another because it's built into our genetic makeup. We've been conditioned to look and act a certain way to attract a compatible mate so that we can one day have children who then will have children, and so on. I believe if our actions come from ancestral conditioning, we can probably change them. We can break the cycle and create unity and support for each other rather than see ourselves as competition for one another.

By the way, I'm not talking about healthy competition. Healthy competition is when we show up to do things we enjoy, and we give them our best shot. There is usually a "winner" and a "loser" (gosh, I hate that L word) at the end of a competition. And that's OK. We win, we lose. Sometimes we get it right and sometimes we don't. It's called *life*. It's called *reality*. It's called *learning*. Stop beating yourself up when you don't get something right. If you knew how many times I have messed up in my life and looked like a complete idiot you'd feel so much better about yourself.

Let us model our ancestors who worked and lived as one to raise their children together. The African proverb "It takes a village to raise a child" couldn't be more beautiful or more accurate. None of us can succeed or stand up to all the pressures in our lives without support.

The question is: How are we as individual sisters choosing to show up? Are we obsessed with our looks, are we jealous, are we looking for approval from the world, are we shaming another because she is succeeding, is our success never good enough, are the words we speak and the thoughts we think rooted in hurt, pain or fear? Are we repeating patterns of hatred and insecurity that have been passed down for generations or are we turning to our peer groups to feel wanted, loved, and accepted? Do you feel good when you "cast a stone" at your friend? Does it feel good when someone does this to you? Are you so numb to the pain that you've stopped hearing or feeling it?

That last one was me. I just shut it all out when people were unkind to me. I denied it was happening. I don't want to do that anymore. I want to embrace my faults and love other women for being human, just like me.

So many women are hurting right now. One of our sisters is staring in the mirror hating her reflection. She is crying over a text she got. Her friend has betrayed her. She was unfriended or unfollowed. She didn't get the promotion. She didn't get the grade. She didn't get the medal. Her partner cheated. She didn't get the guy. She didn't receive the love back that she bravely put out. She put herself out there, only to experience rejection.

She was criticized. She doesn't think she can go on. She is ashamed of her past. She is ashamed of her present. She is uncertain about tomorrow. She is broken and doesn't know how to put it all back together. She was just served papers. She is alone raising her babies. She hates her job. She lost a job she loved. She has family that won't talk to her or shames her. She just yelled at her kids because she's at her breaking point. Or she doesn't speak to her kids. She feels she is never enough.

SHE IS US.

WE ARE HER.

For every woman who has experienced a hard life, there you will find a woman who overcame it and is thriving. She recognized her pain and didn't fall victim to it. She found her way. Usually, all we need is a story from another who has overcome the same thing to lift us and remind us that we are better than our circumstances, stronger. These pivotal moments in our lives allow us to teach others when our friends or strangers face uncertainty or fear. Sharing our stories, wrapping our arms around each other, words of encouragement and kindness can sometimes be the very thing that pulls us from the pain and into our power.

Below is a story I pulled from James Clear's website. We can all relate.

There was an anthropologist who had been studying the habits and culture of a remote African tribe. He had been working in the village for quite some time, and the day before he was to return home, he put together a gift basket filled with delicious fruits from around the region and wrapped it in a ribbon. He placed the basket under a tree, and then he gathered up the children in the village.

The man drew a line in the dirt, looked at the children, and said, "When I tell you to start, run to the tree and whoever gets there first will win the basket of the fruit."

When he told them to run, they all took each other's hands and ran together to the tree. Then they sat together around the basket and enjoyed their treat as a group. The anthropologist was shocked. He asked why they would all go together when one of them could have won all the fruits for themselves.

A young girl looked up at him and said, "How can one of us be happy if all the other ones are sad?"

It's a great question: How can one of us be happy if all of us are sad? How beautiful. How honest. How lovely it would be if we could see our reflections in one another and surround our sister with love if we know that she is hurting. We should send her love. We should tell her she is going to be okay and uplift her. We should remind one another of who we are when we forget.

Because we all do forget at times: We forget that we are made to create and become whatever our hearts desire. May we begin to trust this, even during times and circumstances that are hard to handle? Even through tragedy. Even through periods of pain.

Sometimes we have to go through a storm to see a rainbow. Beauty is the flip side of pain. As long as we are having this human experience, pain will always be a part of our growth and transformation. Like it or not, it is what it is. So be gentle, my dear. Be gentle. Be kind to yourself. Be kind to your sister.

We must begin to take responsibility for our actions and for how we show up. A great place to start this journey is to stop pointing fingers. Remember, when you point a finger at someone else you have three of your fingers pointing right back at you.

Can we all accept that a woman in our lives has hurt us and that we have hurt another woman? In this workbook, I intend for us to peel back some layers of pain. I'm not saying it's going to be easy. It may get muddy. But I also know that the Lotus grows in the mud and you are a beautiful flower, sweet sister. This book has been placed in your hands to remind you of that. So, let's get to work.

 Heartwork

1. When was the last time you hurt yourself? Maybe it was something you said to yourself.

_____

_____

_____

_____

_____

_____

2. Does it feel good to hurt yourself?

_____

_____

_____

_____

_____

3. Why do you keep doing what you know hurts you?

_____

_____

_____

_____

_____

_____

_____

_____

_____

4. What can you begin to do when you find yourself inflicting hurt on your mind, body, or soul?

5. Do you recall a time that you were hurt by another woman? What happened?

6. How did you feel?

_____

_____

_____

_____

_____

_____

_____

7. How did you handle it?

_____

_____

_____

_____

_____

_____

_____

8. How long did the pain last?

_____

_____

_____

_____

_____

_____

_____

_____

9. Did you engage in gossip with other women to make yourself feel better?

_____

_____

_____

_____

_____

_____

10. Did you get depressed or feel worse about your-
self after talking negatively about a sister?

_____

_____

_____

_____

_____

_____

11. Did your pain affect your schoolwork or your
performance at work?

_____

_____

_____

_____

_____

_____

12. Did you obsess over the situation or person that hurt you?

_____

_____

_____

_____

_____

_____

13. Do you still feel the pain when you think about it or her?

_____

_____

_____

_____

_____

_____

14. When have you hurt another woman?

_____

_____

_____

_____

_____

_____

_____

15. What did you do?

_____

_____

_____

_____

_____

_____

_____

_____

16. Did you engage other women in the drama?

_____

_____

_____

_____

_____

_____

_____

17. Did you ever resolve the situation or apologize for being hurtful?

_____

_____

_____

_____

_____

18. How is the relationship today?

_____

_____

_____

_____

19. Does the relationship need healing?

_____

_____

_____

_____

20. Do you still feel pain from doing what you did?

_____

_____

_____

_____

_____

_____

⚬⚭⚬

Now that you have looked at how you may have hurt yourself, been hurt by another woman, and/or hurt another woman, we will do an exercise designed to help you cut the cord from the pain you feel about these circumstances. With this exercise, you may be able to release the pain of being hurt and hurting someone in one sitting, or it may take multiple sessions of doing this exercise to release all the pain.

Use this process for as many days, weeks, or months as it takes.

There are many ways to heal, and everyone is a little different in how they need to do it. Most importantly, I want you to TRUST yourself and what you are ready to do. Sometimes the hardest thing to do is the very thing you need. If you feel significant resistance to doing the current exercise, you may need to finish reading this book first before taking the steps below. Honor your process and promise me that you will eventually work on it.

Let's begin.

Sit in a quiet space at the same time each day if possible.

Close your eyes and take seven deep breaths. Inhale through your nose and exhale through your mouth. Slowly.

Now, keeping your eyes closed, imagine you have a third eye between your eyebrows. Focus on that point with your eyes closed.

Next, I want you to see a person or situation that happened to you or is happening to you. Feel the pain that you or the other person or the situation brings to you and imagine a long golden ribbon that leads from you to her. Imagine she is standing quite a ways from you. You can see all the emotions and fear that you experience and that she experiences between you.

Then, see yourself taking a big pair of golden scissors and cutting the ribbon that links you to the other woman or to the situation. See the person or situation float away happily. Effortlessly. Send her your best wishes. Smile as you release your pain. Thank her for being your teacher and thank yourself for being hers.

Notice if you have begun to feel lighter because you are no longer carrying the weight of painful feelings. Notice you are no longer holding onto what isn't serving you.

Simply let go and be present.

Whenever you are ready, take a few deep breaths and then open your eyes. Go about your day or evening as you usually would.

As I said before, practice this technique every day until you feel like you have released what no longer serves you. Although it may sound odd to you to cut an energy ribbon, I am confident it will work for you as it has for many women.

Don't get frustrated if you don't feel relief right away. You will get the results exactly when you are

ready to get them. Even if it takes months, keep at
it.

If you cry, that's okay. Let the tears fall. You
are not that pain.

2 UNDERSTANDING OUR WOUNDED CHILD

HOW WAS THE HEARTWORK YOU did at the end of Chapter 1? Were there tears? Anger? Resentment? Fear? What came up for you is exactly what needed to occur for personal growth to begin. I am so proud of you for doing the work. You are so freaking fabulous! I love a woman who loves to work on herself. Self-reflection is some of the greatest work you will ever do in your life. Starting here leads you to the place where your heart opens up and true joy can consistently permeate your life.

When we realize that hurt people hurt people, we can empathize with them and show them compassion. At a retreat I attended where the spiritual teacher Marianne Williamson was the guest speaker, a woman asked how to handle someone who has been very hurtful and difficult. Marianne responded, "Realize that it is a cry for love. Imagine them as a small child that you are holding, and they are crying on your shoulder. Energetically send them love every day as you imagine this and watch what happens."

Hearing these words, I felt as though she were speaking directly to me. At that time, I was dealing with a challenging relationship. No matter what I had tried it didn't work. Running away from the person and problem only made it worse. So, I practiced this technique for five days straight. Amazingly, after that fifth day I received a phone call from the person who had been troubling me and it was as if nothing had ever happened. She was loving, kind, and sincere. It was a truly magical outcome.

You may be thinking that this suggestion is a little too weird for you. But try it. Just thinking about a person can change the way she treats you. What we feel for people finds its way to them. We are all energetically connected.

Have you ever been thinking about someone and they call you suddenly? This isn't an accident. We are all energy. Connected at the heart. As we hurt the feeling gets sent to others. As we love others can feel that, too. That's why the power of us, as women gathering together, can heal one another and our beautiful world.

Okay let's jump back to understanding our wounded child. Take a bike accident as an example. Depending on how bad it was, you may not want to ride a bike again. Just the thought of a bike may send hormones coursing through your bloodstream that tell your brain and body, *DON'T DO IT, REMEMBER WHAT HAPPENED LAST TIME.* As a result, you can come to associate pain with something that used to bring you pleasure.

When you were first learning to ride, you wanted to be like other kids. They were having fun laughing and connecting with one another. You wanted that too! Even if you fell off, you'd get up and get right back on that bike. You wanted to join your friends, so you kept practicing to get good at riding the bike. But maybe fear of your past crashes and being scared that a really bad one would happen subsequently kept you from mastering riding a bike.

Fear not. We've all been there, if not with a bike, then with something else. It's hard to realize the fear boiling up is just our minds trying to protect us from something in the past.

When I was nineteen, I was driving with my boyfriend from Phoenix to Sedona. When we left

Arizona, it was 70 degrees and I did not anticipate the massive temperature drop to below freezing as we entered the mountains of California. The car hit a patch of ice, sending us spinning into the mountain where just a couple hundred feet away was a cliff. To say I was scared is an understatement. For a long time, I kept replaying what could have happened, and even up to this day when driving on a mountain I can feel the fear boil up. If my husband or kids are driving, I feel fear for them.

I've had to really work on that wounded teenager inside of me who had the original experience. How I feel today about driving is way better than it was for sure, but I never understood how to heal it and it became a bigger fear. I have learned to temper my fear by reminding myself that the universe is working for me, never against me. And that all that happens, happens for my highest good! Whenever I feel afraid now behind the wheel, I breathe through it and focus on what I should be grateful for.

How does fear show up in our relationships with other women? If we've ever been the subject of gossip or participated in gossiping about a girl or woman behind her back, then we may be wary of being too vulnerable in female company? We may keep our guard up so that nobody can find something to "use against us." We can fear judgment, criticism, bullying, putdowns, especially if our self-esteem is not robust. But we need to remember that often these types of meanspirited attacks come from a woman or girl trying to deflect attention away from her own supposed flaws and vulnerabilities. She may be experiencing deep-rooted pain from having had someone hurt her in the same way. She may never have learned to love herself.

It's easier to push people away than to draw them closer. Also, if we do not have appropriate role models at home to show us how to handle adversity and struggle in a loving and open way, we often are not strong enough to figure things out on our own. Our job is not to try and save people, nor is it to be friends with everyone. Some people just don't want that, but we can express kindness and love and likely diminish the threat you may be to them.

How do we do that, you ask. I can't only tell you what's worked for me and maybe it will resonate for you. If you back an angry dog into a corner, he will bite you. A happy dog won't do that. We can practice that with our sisters. Gossiping and getting your friends to send negative energy to a backed-in-the-corner woman will just make her defensive.

Instead, try gathering your sisters. Put out a bowl and have everyone in the group write down the name of a woman or girl they know who needs good vibes. No one even needs to know their names. Just the group consciousness of everybody together gathered to spread good vibes will help the situation change over time. Do this instead of feeding the negativity. And don't be afraid to throw your own name into the bowl as well if you need some extra love.

Some may call this "prayer" and to keep this book universally embraced by all, I will leave it up to you and the members of your Gather Group to call it whatever you want. For now, let's call this activity the Good Vibes Bowl.

When you deal with a *frenemy* (a friend who can be a little malicious at times behind your back or someone who is pretending to be a friend and isn't) or even a difficult family member, show her compassion. Show her kindness because you know the difference. As the late motivational speaker Wayne Dyer used to say, "Change the way you look at things and the things you look at will change." I believe this to be true.

Before we go any further, please heed this caveat. If someone is physically hurting you or you feel like someone may hurt you, get help immediately. Nobody has the right to hit you or call you names. If the unpleasantness you are dealing with is just a display of jealousy or rude behavior, you've got this, beautiful sister. We have a tendency to take people's remarks and behavior personally and to heart. It's so easy to get our feelings hurt if we do not understand the backstory of where a woman or girl is coming from.

Taking a bird's eye view of another woman's life would make you love her more for enduring the pain that she has experienced or which you may imagine she's experienced. Seeing her like this is not about putting yourself above anyone else or even feeling that you're better than anyone, please understand this. It's about sharing a common humanity with other people.

Think how a sister's day might change if you anonymously left your favorite book in her mailbox. Oftentimes a random act of love can change a person forever. A smile is one of the greatest gifts you can share with people, so instead of being glued to your phone all the time choose to be different, to be connected. I dare you. Lift your gaze and look people in the eyes, acknowledge that you see them with a smile. It feels so amazing not to worry how the world will see you. Would you rather be liked or loved? It's a radically peaceful Zen place to be to love.

I'm still working on healing my wounded inner child and I'm in my forties. My mom had me when she was fifteen. We lived in car when I was a kid behind a Pizza Hut off and on. My mother married the manager of the Pizza Hut and we thought we had hit the jackpot. However, life dramatically changed. He was an alcoholic and a drug abuser. As a result, of not knowing how he was going to show up, I felt insecure. I spent most of my childhood living in fear of what was going to come around the next corner. I developed trust issues and I have had to learn not to push away, but to embrace, love and support. This took time.

When you're working to overcome fear, anger, and hurt, you will think you worked through it and something may stir it up and then the works begins again. I do believe it gets better, though. I know for me it has and I feel and live a more authentic and heart-filled life because I have dealt with my wounded inner child.

So many people blame others for their pain. Their struggle. Some are vocal about it and some like to just keep the struggle nearby as if it was their friend. Sometimes people get love and connection if they use their wounded child as an excuse as to why they behaved a certain way or why people should feel sorry for them. This is a sign of someone whose wounded child needs attention. When my boys were little, my boys acted out when I worked too much and didn't give them enough attention. They'd fight with each other and purposely did things they knew would get them in trouble. I finally figured out that all they wanted was some attention and love. So, I started turning off my phone and not working for one hour a day. During that hour I would play with them or take them to the park, and it would be all about them time. They just wanted time with me and to feel my attention, they didn't care if they were getting negative or positive attention.

I still see adults do this. That part of their wounded child comes out and they don't realize that giving loving attention to yourself and then focusing on caring for others will make them feel so much better and will not make them feel alone. I can only share my truth from my experiences from my pain and struggle to joy and love. We live in a selfie society and I do it too. But I don't do selfies to get more likes on Instagram or Facebook, I do it to share a story or an experience. I do it so that people receive a gift from me. Every day when I work on social media, I'm always thinking, *What can I share that will lift other people up?*

Now let's do some wounded inner child heartwork, my friend. Turn the page.

Heartwork

1. Was there ever something that happened to you that left you feeling alone, abandoned, never good enough, or unworthy of love?

_____

_____

_____

_____

_____

2. Does your memory of this event continue to haunt you, and if so, when does it show up?

_____

_____

_____

_____

_____

3. What would you say to the child you were when this happen to comfort her and help her feel better?

_____

_____

_____

_____

_____

_____

_____

4. Did a parent, friend, family member, teacher, or anyone you look up to say or do something to you that caused you pain and or shame?

_____

_____

_____

_____

_____

_____

CHRISTY DREILING

5. How did you feel when this happened?

_____

_____

_____

_____

_____

_____

6. What do you wish you had heard from this person instead that would have made you feel good about yourself, proud, and beautiful?

_____

_____

_____

_____

_____

Please take a moment to put a hand on your heart and say those words to yourself now. If there is a mirror nearby, go to the mirror and look into your eyes and say those kind words again.

• 42 •

Remember, you do not have to share your writing with anyone. But you do need to trust yourself and be honest with yourself to work on yourself. Dance with your hurt for your own good. For your healing. For your transformation. It won't necessarily be easy, but it will be worth it.

3 SUPERWOMAN SYNDROME

HAVE YOU NOTICED THAT YOU FEEL more and more overwhelmed? Do you feel like the world is resting on your shoulders? Maybe you're a student and you feel pressure to "get the grade" or you're a mom and you feel the pressure to be the "perfect PTA (or PTO) mom." Perhaps you work a corporate job or even own a business, but you still feel the pressure to be the best. You try to hit all the deadlines and never drop any of the many balls that you are juggling. Maybe you feel like you are being left behind because you are not keeping up. Some thoughts that may go through your head are:

I don't want to let them down.

I don't want to be a failure.

I don't want to be a bad mom.

I don't want to be a bad wife.

Do your thoughts then spiral to thought like these?

What will they think of me?

What if they think I'm not good enough?

What if they tell me I told you so or even deny me their love because I'm not meeting their expectations?

More and more women and girls put expectations of perfection on themselves and even more so on each other. I have done it to myself and I have placed expectations on others as well. This may be a touchy subject for you right now. If you're not ready to change this behavior, perhaps you will feel safe enough to take a small step toward turning off the pressure cooker inside because that's exactly what it is. A pressure cooker that can only take so much before it blows. The same holds true for a person.

It's okay to have some grit. To be persistent and work hard. Grit makes the world flourish and great things get done. We're not talking about that. We're talking about perfectionism for its own sake. We're talking about those of us who are so busy and have so overwhelmed ourselves that we've stopped living. Stopped laughing. Stopped having fun. Stopped working on ourselves because we don't have time for that.

Can we all just take off our Superwoman capes for a moment and try to imagine living in a world together where when we feel stressed and overwhelmed, we ask for help without thinking this means we're weak? When we feel stressed can we take a load off without feeling guilty for doing self-nurturing? When we're scared or confused, can we ask for help from a sister without fearing she's going to go spread gossip or look at us differently?

Redefining what it means to be a Superwoman may be a good place to start. Here's my new definition: To be a Superwoman means that we are kind, conscientious, bold when we need to be, calm when the storm is near, and gentle when we're pushed to the edge. We take responsibility for assuming our place in the world and the contribution we are making in it.

For years I was driven by fear. Fear that I would go back to being hungry. Fear of living a deprived life like I did as a child. Fear of losing it, being judged, never being good enough or accepted, and not being loved. I chased fame, recognition, and success, and then I chased more. I was working in overdrive to get ahead to numb myself and avoid feeling my hurt. My pain. Trying to prove to myself and to the world that I was worthy to exist.

Standing on a stage with thousands of women and men cheering for me, many times I stood there thinking, *I hope they never figure out how weak I truly am or what a failure I have been.* I started to hide from my heroic inner self, so people wouldn't know I was losing it. I thought that if I earned the title and the car, had the money in the bank, built the big fancy house in the country, or traveled and showed it to the public on Instagram and Facebook then I would have finally made it and abandoned or outgrown my past. But the dark night of the soul fell upon me and I had to go within and heal. It was obvious that I kept chasing an image I had imagined in my mind for most of my life when I was actually searching for love.

The problem was not making money or being influential. It was being those things and doing what I did to create them in my life for the wrong reasons. I am not anti-abundance or anti-earning or anti-work. I love abundance and I will teach you how to love it as well. But I'm for it for all the right reasons—for the power of being able to take care of my family and be generous with people who need uplifting.

Let's not get love in all the wrong places. True authentic love comes from loving ourselves and from loving the beauty we find in others and the world around us as well. Without condition. I believe it's super important to have goals and dreams and to chase them. The carrots dangled before our eyes are different for each of us. But the result of reaching out and catching those carrots is the same. If we believe catching what we've chased will fulfill us, we may be let down because real fulfillment comes from within.

I want to help you to remove your burdens, reduce your stress, and eliminate overwhelm. If you seek transformation, evolution, growth, and contribution, the byproducts of all of that will be more freedom to express yourself and to live your life the way you visualize or dream.

I love to travel. I love beautiful environments. I love taking trips with my family. I love being able to choose daily where I want to spend my time. I love being able to give back where I want to give back in the ways I choose to. I freaking love my life because I am honoring my spirit's calling for growth and community. But this is new.

I used to be so afraid of the money I earned that I would try to get rid of it as fast as I got it. Who was I to deserve a lifestyle of no struggle and pain? That was all I knew. My comfort zone was "hardness" and "struggle." I kept creating new problems to overcome so I could get a hit of accomplishment from finding a solution. Sounds like an addiction, doesn't it? The trouble is, it wasn't making me happy.

When we believe that more money and more fame will bring us the joy we are searching for, we are mistaken, so we are setting ourselves up for disappointment. These things just are not the source of happiness. But we may need to experience this truth in order to understand that.

I encourage you to dig deep and really be okay with where you are and the journey you are on. I myself feel I had to go through what I went through to become who I am and to get to a place of true personal freedom. I wouldn't change any of it except for the shaming of myself that I did during and after it all. We must just love ourselves where and how we are. And love working on loving ourselves through whatever we are going through.

Painting visualizations in our mind's eye of who we want to become or the reality we want to live in is necessary for calling that thing into existence and attracting it to come to us. Not measuring a woman by her bank accounts or fame is a part of growth as a human being. If we can see her as worthy, then we can see ourselves as worthy. A woman should be recognized for the beauty that exists inside her. For the artist she chooses to be. For the growth she has experienced. Sometimes our minds are so programmed that we can't even see that our programs are faulty or hindering our development. A big one that gets in the way is thinking we aren't deserving or intelligent if we're not overflowing with cash at every moment.

How can you gauge if you're being run by a faulty program? Well, I would ask you if similar negative circumstances keep repeating? Do you often wonder why the same something always happens to you? Life throws lessons our way for us to learn from. Observing patterns is how you can grow and evolve. Right now, you are reading this because it's time for you to awaken inside and really begin to start living on purpose instead of trying to get by and just praying and wishing you don't have a bad day.

It's not enough to hide out and hope that something negative doesn't show up to take you off your course. You can be sure there will be something you need to manage to stay focused. We feel like we're hiding until we accept that life "will happen" and problems "will pop up." I used to run from painful situation too until I started working on "how I would react" when they did show up. And of course, there are some thing that are so devastating that you can't predict how you will react. Prepare for these by knowing you could need a break to regroup.

I lost my former best friend. We had a falling out and she died before we could repair our relationship. She was truly the best friend I've ever had and I pushed her away. A year later, a good friend took his life and my greatest grandfather passed away. Then one year after that, my father unexpectedly passed away at the age of fifty-nine. We had been closer than ever and had just come off of a father-daughter trip where we healed a lot of wounds. Some people may think that after all of this that I would be in a funk. I had bad days, really hard curled-up-in-a-ball days, but I kept saying to myself, *The universe has my back and everything happens for the greater good.* I was determined to run positive programs in my mind and choose how I would respond so I would not be bitter.

I decided to use my pain, my story, to help others.

The big truth is that we all struggle. We all have pain and hardship, but it's an option whether to let it build us or break us. We get to decide. Sometimes we choose to be broken but we can always choose to be built back up stronger and better than ever. We get to choose.

After those terrible three years with those terrible losses, I asked myself what I truly wanted. What did I love and what made me smile the most?

My habit of letting fear take the driver's seat and never really taking time to explore my soul's callings and cravings was a habit I was prepared to break.

I asked myself, *Am I doing this because I feel obligated? Does that bring me happiness? Is this in alignment with my values? Do I feel elevated around that person? Do I really want to live here for the rest of my life? Where have I not explored that I want to explore? What else is possible?*

As a result of my self-inquiry, I found myself on a new road with pain, drama, fear, fame, and so much more fading in the distance behind me. I stood before a beautiful clear, golden path before me filled with the opportunity to design, create, discover, and uncover who I am.

I asked: Who am I really if fear is not driving me? Who am I really if people's perceptions of me aren't defining me? Who am I really when I don't let my past hold me back from designing my life exactly as I want? This meant challenging all the things I thought were my reality or true. This led to doing the unexpected, like my family and me deciding to pick up, leave Kansas, and move to the West Coast. If that wasn't really putting it all behind us, I don't know what would be. It was time for reinvention and the ignition of our souls.

When we made the announcement, people didn't even believe us. Few were excited for us. Very few. See, we had recently built a gorgeous dream home on nineteen acres. We'd been there less than four years. By the time we left, the house had not sold yet. But we knew we had to go. You know, you really learn a lot about people when you make a drastic change in your life. The family and friends who were high-fiving us and saying they would be coming to visit showed their truth and warmed my soul. Then we drove three vehicles and a U-Haul with two dogs and two cats across country embracing the adventure to meet our fate. It was exciting. I felt like I was singing my own song and the world was exploding in color and vibrancy.

Shouldn't we all be exploring ourselves and listening for the sounds of our songs? We often listen to other people's songs, and sometimes we try to sing their songs and make their songs our own, but then the rhythm is off. What if your song is waiting for you to sing it? What is more flavor, more vibrant color is waiting for you?

Yes, it takes courage to stop doing what others are doing and to do what you've never done. You may fail but at least you will know you tried. That you stepped into fully embodying yourself. You, beautiful child. Yes, I am calling you a child, no matter what your age. Because there is still that child in you who yearns for attention. Who wants you to come and play. Who wants to laugh and explore.

Why do we silence the inner child for so long? Why didn't we let her sing her song—teach us her song? Because we took on the responsibility of growing up.

You've heard a parent say, "Just grow up." We all have. I believe I said that to my kids in their teens not knowing what I was really saying. I would say something like, "You are thirteen now, it's time you start acting like it." My boys must have looked at me like I had three eyes. What is THAT supposed to mean?

Don't get me wrong. I'm not advocating for a lack of responsibility. Being responsible for our space in the world and how we treat ourselves, others, and our planet is what conscious people do and if we all were a bit more conscious, we wouldn't have as much suffering as we have now. I'm advocating for you to be responsible for making your own life fulfilling.

So, my sweet sister. What can you put down that isn't serving you?

Something more than cleaning or doing the dishes, I mean. These are things we do if we're being conscious of our space and honoring and respecting our surroundings. To leave everything unkempt is not being conscious. Find ways to make doing those kinds of tasks fun, like turning on music while you do them. Think "gratitude" while you do those things.

While you're doing laundry think, *I am so grateful that I have clothes to wear. I am so grateful I could purchase this clothing. I am so grateful that these shoes and pants and shirts provides comfort as I wear them.* Program your mind to appreciate what you have.

Yet, there are things you can leave behind to make room for something better. Let's do some work here now to discover these.

Heartwork begin on the next page.

Heartwork

1. What do you do currently in your life that you do not like to do (your job, volunteer work, hanging out with people whom you don't want to hang with, a certain type of exercise)?

_____

_____

_____

_____

_____

_____

_____

_____

_____

_____

2. Why do you do it?

_____

_____

_____

_____

_____

_____

3. How do you feel when you think about not doing it, heavy or light? If you feel lighter, which means a weight has been lifted off of you, then this is a sign from your emotional guidance system that doing it is not in alignment with your soul.

_____

_____

_____

_____

_____

_____

4. What would you rather do to replace it? This is about naming options. For example, if you don't like running, which you've been doing to stay fit, you could try hiking or doing Zumba.

---

5. If you belong to a Gather Group, go around the circle of sisters and have participants share insights about what they would like to stop doing and what they could do instead—if anything. Every woman should also get a chance to practice saying "No thanks."

Please be aware that your sisters' job is to listen to you and be a witness as you get clear about your vision for your life, and your job is to play the same role for her. As supportive women, we don't need to convince anyone to do anything. Rather, we should encourage each sister to trust that she herself knows deep down what her soul yearns for.

4 DIFFERENT IS BEAUTIFUL

HAVE YOU EVER FOUND YOURSELF talking with someone when she says something that turns you off? Maybe she doesn't have the same religious or spiritual belief as you. Maybe she is a member of a different political party than you. Maybe she went to a rival school or has different parenting beliefs or beliefs in general? I have found myself on both sides of this fence. Having said something that is not liked and not liking what I'm hearing being said. Being kind and polite, but then disconnecting because the woman does not think like me. We all have quite strong beliefs and opinions. We tend to choose friends and networks that way, don't we?

Over the last few years, I have really challenged myself to step into others' perceptual worldview to understand what they see. To understand why they believe what they believe and do what they do. To know their story. To connect with their hearts. Understanding other people's intention has become my priority. This does not mean I become everybody's best friend. It just means I respect them as beings and because I do, it gives me permission to respect myself.

I encourage you to explore the minds and hearts of people around you who are different from you. Often, the people who dare to be different are people who will change the world.

If we can listen to one another and share our feelings and beliefs in a nonjudgmental way, we can bridge the gap that we sisters have. This doesn't mean that we need to like what everybody else likes, but being an explorer sure does sound interesting, doesn't it? In the process of listening and learning, you will likely find out so much about your neighbor that you never knew and may realize that your perception of her was likely wrong.

Here are some common misperceptions we have to cope with in our society.

Rich people are mean.

Poor people are lazy.

Women who cry are soft.

Men who cry are soft.

You can't be a great mom and wife, and a great businesswoman.
Girls can't do math or science.
Women are bad at numbers.
It's a man's world.
Women executives are not supportive of other women.
Attractive girls have it easier than the rest.
Attractive girls are not as smart as other girls.
Liberals are more compassionate and sympathetic.
Conservatives are more patriotic and religious.
Atheists worship the devil.

How many times have you listened to gossip about a person only to realize later that none of it was true? How many times have you judged someone because of what she looked like or how she dressed only to realize that this wasn't even relevant to who she was? Years ago, when I was young and a newly successful as an entrepreneur, I went on a shopping spree. I had always dreamed of walking into Pottery Barn and buying curtains or a piece of nice furniture for my home. There was no way that we could have afforded to buy them until this moment. Perhaps I should have dressed up for the occasion, perhaps not, but I was a mom with young kids and I had a lot on my plate. So, into the store I went in my sweatpants and tee-shirt with my kiddos. My middle son was in the stroller and had food dripped all over him from his last snack.

I was so excited. At last I could walk in and purchase whichever curtains I wanted, and I could not wait. But this was a *Pretty Woman* moment for me. The salespeople didn't share my enthusiasm. Although I got in there and I found the very curtains I wanted no one on the sales staff would help me. I finally got the attention of one of the sales associates. She came over smiling, but with reservation expressed in her body language. I told her which curtains I wanted, and instead of immediately leaping into action to get them for me, she said, "Ma'am, those are two-hundred-and-fifty dollars" in a tone that implied, *"You must not know how expensive those are."* I could feel anger literally hurt boiling up inside me.

In my mind, I was trying to decide if I should just walk out. I hated being judged but I really wanted those curtains. So instead I said, "Yep, those are the exact ones I want." Then she changed from being annoyed by me to trying to show me everything else in the store.

Sadly, this hasn't been the only time when I have been perceived differently because of the clothes I've been wearing or the car I was driving. I'll tell you one more story because I could go on for days about this. I was told in high school by some peers that all I would ever be was a "stupid model" after I had shared that I wanted to one day become an entertainment lawyer. I remember the tears of embarrassment I held back in the classroom after I was being teased. Well, my ten-year class reunion was coming up and I had just purchased a brand-new G Wagon Mercedes. If you don't know the model, all you need to know is it is a top-of-the-line car. I wanted so badly to drive up in my brand new G Wagon to make my point that I was better than the people who had looked down on me and made demeaning comments. I had worked my tail off to earn that car. I mean, I worked hard! I knew the kids who had laughed at me were going to be there.

When I showed up at my reunion in the new car, I could feel the same guys who laughed at me feeling less than me. Although they spoke about their cars not being as great as mine it didn't actually make me feel proud of myself. For some reason making them feel the way they had made me feel back in high school didn't feel good at all. That's because comparing people because of money is a false measurement of their worth as human beings. Also, I learned that when we shoot an arrow at someone else, we have the same arrow come back to us.

Furthermore, on some level I am grateful to those guys because they motivated me. The pain I went through from being put down was a catalyst for my growth! It pushed me to try harder. Sometimes I believe the universe sends us just what we need to get us fired up. But if we don't use pain as rocket fuel then we may fall into the trap that most people fall into believing that the perceptions others have of us are reality. Believing what people say means giving your control away. You know that, right? Stop giving your control away to meanspirited people who do not even deserve a second of your attention.

I like to compare critical thoughts in the mind to the weeds in a garden. One day, you see flowers and the beautiful reflection of God's beauty staring back at you, then you forget to tend to the garden for a few days and the weeds creep in and take over! Weeds are a nuisance. These are the types of thoughts that inflict pain on us—and also cause us to criticize one another and act like those kids in my high school.

Pull these weeds daily, because if you don't, they will take over your garden.

My sons have called me out a few times when I was out of line in my comments to somebody. I have always taught them to be kind, telling them, "That server you're talking to could be your boss one day or become the next Steve Jobs, you never know." I believe we all need to imagine this potential in people because it helps us behave respectfully. Everybody deserves respect and to be treated with dignity.

That said, I have had bad moments. Maybe when service I received was super horrible or a telemarketer was relentless. Then I acted out of character and made some obnoxious remarks. And my boys called me out. A few times I have gone so far as calling someone I've hung up on back and apologizing for my reaction because I wanted to model for my boys that we are human and we make mistakes. If we do, we can apologize. There is no reason to shame ourselves for our mistakes, but we will teach each other so much more by saying, "Sorry, please forgive me," than just walking or running away and beating ourselves up for our reactions—or even worse justifying our poor behavior by beating up other people in our minds for just doing their jobs.

The title of my last book was *LOL,* not because I wrote a funny book. To me, the meaning of the acronym LOL has always been "lots of love." Years ago, a friend called me out for signing an email I sent him with LOL. He rang me up and asked, "Christy, what was so funny?" I replied, "Bob, I didn't mean for anything to be funny, but I do send you lots of love." He started laughing and said, "Christy, LOL doesn't mean 'lots of love,' it means 'laugh out loud.'" "Oh no," I said. "Bob, I have signed every email and text with LOL for eight years!" We laughed and laughed and then I realized the impact of perception.

I mentored lots of women over those years and my emails have gone something like this, "Hey Jan, you are one bright and brilliant woman and I know you can overcome any obstacle you set your mind to overcoming, LOL." Imagine the humiliation and hurt feelings that may have caused. I was trying to bolster their self-esteem and yet I was signaling it was a joke? Even so. Before Bob, nobody ever asked me about it. If they had hurt feelings, they swallowed them. I share this story around the world because I feel it's important that we question our feelings. Why did it take eight years for a *man* to ask me what I meant? All these women for all these years may have felt uneasy or upset but none questioned me or helped me out by setting me straight.

If you have ever perceived a look, a comment, or a lack of a comment from someone in your social circles as having a negative implication, especially if it is from someone who is usually friendly and supportive, I recommend that you assume the best rather than the worst. We can create these big stories in our heads that are super dramatic and painful for us and we can get angry and hurt by the stories. But we need to put out these five-alarm fires before we let them burn us down. Our thoughts can set off explosions that destroy us and everyone else around us.

Choosing to assume the best is a mental discipline that takes patience to master. We have to work on breaking the habit of negative assumptions too. People debate how long it takes to form a new habit. Some say twenty-eight days, some say thirty. Let's say it's thirty and be gentle on ourselves if we don't break through right away to a new way of being.

The truth is that we will always be working on ourselves. When we stop working on ourselves then we stop growing. We all know what the opposite of growth is—contraction. The best work you will ever do is the work on yourself and how you react to the world you live in.

When I was in the fifth grade, my best friend and I were at the swimming pool. She put her ankles together and said, "See this, if your thighs don't touch then that means you're skinny." I put mine together and my thighs touched. From that day on for years, I would stand in front of the mirror and see if my legs touched and I thought I was fat because they did. One idea kept me from looking in the mirror for most of my life and seeing beauty in my body. The shape of my ankles kept me from seeing a girl who could do anything her heart desired.

And imagine the impact on me of being called "poor white trash" by my peers, because my family was not affluent. *Trash* means "garbage," the stuff you throw away. I was also called stupid, dense, and not smart because I did beauty pageants and earned money modeling. Had people known I was fighting for my survival, would they have been so cruel or thought better of me? My mom had to use "fake money" (food stamps) to buy groceries. I found this embarrassing and would always scout out which teen baggers were working so I would know if I needed to tell my mom I was going to the car early or not.

Poverty is tough. When the old car wouldn't start, we would have to run and push it to get it going. We made Christmas presents for each other by hand because we had absolutely nothing to give. Our house windows in the winter were covered in plastic wrap and duct tape to keep out the cold air. On really frosty mornings, we would go to the kitchen and turn on the stove to warm up. My mom really did the best she could. But despite it all, poverty affected my thinking—and I really had to purposefully work on how I thought to break the habit of believing that the awful names I was called were true in any way, shape, or form.

As women, we should come together and lift one another up. We are all struggling in some way with our own darkness, perhaps from a past trauma or insecurities. No one is immune to negativity. Even people who look like they have it all together have times that they don't feel so great about themselves. We all do! And this is when having a sisterhood of support can be powerful. We can let each other know that we are smart, beautiful, competent, and lovable.

I love helping people. I love watching their lives change. I love it so much that it is a big part of why I am successful in my job. My joy doesn't come from being compensated financially and balancing my checkbook. It comes from smiles. It comes from being a hope dealer.

Another misperception I have had to work on is thinking that people with money are bad. I really felt conflicted by this idea because when I started making money in my profession as a coach, it caught up with me. I realized I had spent most of my life in a struggle and I was sabotaging my newfound certainty by falling into the same patterns of needing to struggle to earn respect, success, love, and attention. I sabotaged myself and did things to lose the money. But I worked on my thought patterns and I finally caught on to my broken pattern. I had spent forty years of my life buying into the lie about needing to struggle and prove myself deserving of what I earned and then I broke free of these ideas and that way of living.

Now I'm committed to spending the rest of my life offering my light, my experience, and my story in the hope that I can encourage not one, not two, but millions of women, including thousands of young women and girls, to support each other and counteract the negative voices in their own heads, lend advice, and offer their kindness when the storm clouds of life roll in. While you're reading this book, please accept my challenge to uplift the women you know.

Go to the next page.

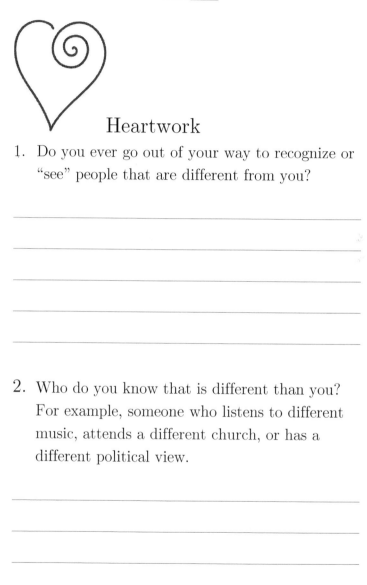

Heartwork

1. Do you ever go out of your way to recognize or "see" people that are different from you?

_____

_____

_____

_____

_____

2. Who do you know that is different than you? For example, someone who listens to different music, attends a different church, or has a different political view.

_____

_____

_____

_____

_____

_____

3. What are some ways you can start to open up
   your heart to seeing this woman? Could you
   smile? Start a conversation? Invite her to coffee?

_____

_____

_____

_____

_____

_____

_____

⚬⚭⚬

It's important that you do not try and "change"
others. Be a great listener and truly be interested in
their life. Listen to your thoughts. Are you judging
them? Why? Where does that come from? Did you
have a parent or close relative or friend who held a
judgment or was afraid of someone different than
them? Remember that we have been conditioned by
our environments. The homes we live in, the towns
where we live, the churches and synagogues we go
to, the family gatherings, the educations we are
given. If you were born in a completely different

household opposite of yours, you would likely be molded by some or all the ideas and messages you received growing up.

This is why I believe that we must constantly be reinventing ourselves and it's so important to travel and explore the world. Eat new foods, experiences new places, dare to dream! How are you to know if you never leave the nest. But be prepared, those who have never left the nest may feel threatened by your interest in growth and discovery. They may try to pull you back. This isn't because they don't love you. They just don't know what they don't know.

Now is an important time in your life to begin to question everything you have every been taught and ask, *Does this feel good?* My rule of thumb is to always make sure that whatever I am doing or saying leads to a positive impact for all involved.

5 LOVE BOUNDARIES

WE HAVE A CHOICE IN each and every moment to focus either on love or fear. To protect us, it is common for the mind to make up stories that go against what we desire. For example, if you want to ask your boss for a raise or telling a man you've been secretly in love with him for years, your head might fill with images of the conversation going poorly. However, because our minds are so programmable, whatever we feed them in the way of thoughts gets mirrored back to us in additional imagery from our imagination. The negative imagery is fear feeding on anxiety of taking a risk. This tendency is why you will always hear me talking about "minding your mind." By this I mean feeding the mind with positive programs through tools such as affirmations. *I look in the mirror and I love the girl I see. Each and every day she is getting better and better,* is a phrase I like to repeat to myself mentally as I am brushing my teeth in the morning. And by surrounding ourselves with positive-thinking, supportive people whose comments uplift us.

What can we do when the people around us hold us back from our dreams by instilling our minds with negative, fearful imagery or put us down so often that we begin to believe we don't have what it takes to succeed or we're not lovable and deserving of the best in our lives? We need to establish boundaries that preserve our mental and emotional condition. We need to mind our hearts as well as our heads by recognizing when relationships are crossing lines.

Here is a series of questions designed to help you discern if the boundaries you set *for your own behavior* and the boundaries you set *for the behavior of other people* are not clear enough. Reflect on each for a moment. Use them to spark a conversation in your Gather Group.

- Do you hang on to relationships too long because you feel like you are obligated?
- Do you feel like you have so much time invested in a relationship that you have to

stay the course in order to "be a good person"?

- Do you feel like you're constantly being judged and are never enough?
- Do you feel others competing with you?
- Does anyone try to shame you? For instance, does someone guilt trip you all the time?
- Are you being manipulated to think that you are the one wrong or at fault—perhaps someone who never takes ownership of his own contribution to situations?
- Do you feel suffocated by someone's love? For instance, does someone want to give to you so much that the gifts are smothering?
- Does someone always want to give her opinions to you even when you don't ask?
- Maybe someone is projecting her life onto you and how she thinks your life should be.

While we're on the topic of boundaries, an important thing to understand is that we cannot control others; we can only control ourselves. If you recognize, for instance, that you find it annoying and upsetting to have people constantly critiquing your choices, yet you continue to invite their judgment or seek their approval, then you are the one who needs to change. You need to ask yourself if you are putting yourself in the position of feeling unhappy and awkward every time painful people enter your space. Uncomfortable feelings and gut instincts are your emotional guidance system saying, *Listen to me. Pay attention. Something is wrong here.*

One of my hopes in writing this book is that I am able to teach you to trust your gut more.

Sometimes we have so much negativity programmed into our own minds that we need to express it out loud to someone else in order to see it for what it is and begin to remove it. This is when we as women should come together and lean on one another. We should listen. But be careful not to give advice unless asked. Honoring each other's process of life and learning. We can share our own stories to help our sisters find the best paths for themselves.

I have had many painful experiences. Loss of family. Loss of friends. Boyfriend breakups. Financial hardship. Spiritual warfare. Family warfare. Career setbacks. Emotional setbacks. Depression. Must I go on? Let's just agree that we are all human and we all have experiences and areas in our lives that need some work. We get tested by people, circumstances, or things to get us to wake up and *grow!*

I believe we are all individual trees of life with many branches representing our many experiences.

We start out as little acorns. Looking at an acorn's outer shell, you cannot see the majestic oak hiding inside it. The acorn knows that it will become a large beautiful oak tree one day. Regardless of the weather, it knows its purpose—to grow tall.

Would you like to be as known as an acorn in the process of becoming an oak tree? If so, this requires you to create love boundaries. The tulip bulb does not try and convince the acorn to be a tulip because that is not the purpose of the acorn. This idea seems silly, doesn't it? It is also silly when someone tries to convince us to be something we are not or to do something that is not what we know we are to do. This is where love boundaries come in.

If every time you are with someone you do not feel respected and you feel worse about yourself, this is a signal that your relationship is out of alignment from what your soul hungers for or desires to give and receive with this individual. You need to love yourself enough to investigate the best way to handle this pain.

Is this person open to communication? Does she get defensive? How is she with others? Does she get argumentative or does she listen? Does she show support? Does she have good intentions and a good heart? Some people you can speak to directly and initiate a conversation. With people who get defensive, I've learned that they are often so hurt and angry inside that they can take it as a form of attack even if you go to them with love. With some people it's best to focus on distance healing.

It is important not to fear losing love and connection just because you have boundaries. It is important to know that your voice matters. It needs to be heard, even if someone pushes you away or does not want to share love and connection with you any longer. Do not silence your voice, my sister, because you fear not being heard or because you fear not being loved.

In my view, it is important to speak with love when we know we are someone who simply has not been taught how we prefer to be treated or who has never before been told that their actions are upsetting to us. Assume the best and you can collaborate on finding a solution. Does your voice speak love or does it speak venom? What is the intention behind your voice? What is the intention in someone else's voice? It's all about intention, isn't it?

I'm a huge believer in trying to heal relationships that are worth healing, but I am also not naïve. Some people do not want to heal. They don't want to change. They aren't either ready or willing. It is not our job to try to convince people that they should drink from the well of joy.

By establishing love boundaries inside ourselves, we can be an example to our sisters. Let us be the light. Let us abolish our own fear and darkness. Let us be the dance for someone to see who has been blind. Let us be the voice for those who have lost theirs. Let us be the sound to the song. Our boundaries are our examples.

By this, I mean, for example, that if a woman in our lives acts like a perpetual victim or drama queen, we do not convince her of a different way of being, but we also do not need to engage with her in the drama or the belief in her powerlessness. That can be a boundary. We can change the subject. We can walk away. We can see her in our mind's eye as whole. A drama queen feeds off the negative energy of others. When some unhappy people see happy people, they do whatever it takes to disrupt the joy because it reminds them of the sadness in their own souls. They want to have a "gathering" in a dark sense by multiplying their inner darkness. To "gather" in the light we must choose love, beauty, friendship, fellowship, family, and fun.

Some people get addicted to pain and we see this showing up in all forms. Before I married my husband, I had a boyfriend once who would make fun of my roots. I started feeling embarrassed about where I came from and insecure. His family were the opposite of mine, wealthy and well educated. He was so addicted to maintaining his self-image of perfection that we literally spent two hours every day working on our bodies. If I was about to put food in my mouth that did not meet his standards, he would say things to cause me to feel ashamed.

Even at that young age, I was strong enough to know I didn't want that for the rest of my life. Yet too weak to leave him then and there because if I did it meant I would have to move back to Kansas from Los Angeles, where I pictured everyone looking at me as a failure.

Have you ever stayed somewhere way too long because you worried that you would be judged or considered a failure? Did you ever make up the story that you could feel humiliated by a choice to follow your emotional guidance? This is a perfect example of how a loving boundary needed to be in place in me. If the majority of my time with him was me feeling worse about myself, either our relationship had to change, or I had to change and get out. Which is exactly what I did ultimately. I learned to set a boundary of being more loving to myself.

As a little girl, one of my stepfathers, who was a drug addict and alcoholic, would beat up my mother. His rage was frightening for me and my younger sisters. We would run and hide. One of his tactics afterward was to act kind and loving. Eventually I caught on to what he was doing. His behavior was a form of manipulation to keep my mom hooked on him. Sometimes when we choose to get love and connection from an unhealthy relationship, it's because we are feeling depleted of love. We can avoid putting ourselves in this space by setting our boundaries and being sure to self-nurture so that we do not feel depleted. By knowing what we want.

If you are unsure of what you want in a relationship, you can learn what you want by paying attention to other people's relationships. Hang around people who have positive relationships and compare these to the negative ones you've seen. This will show you what feels good and what doesn't feel good. You do not have to follow the patterns that you have seen growing up just because that is all you know or have witnessed.

Let's set ourselves up for success in our relationships by doing some heartwork now.

Turn the page.

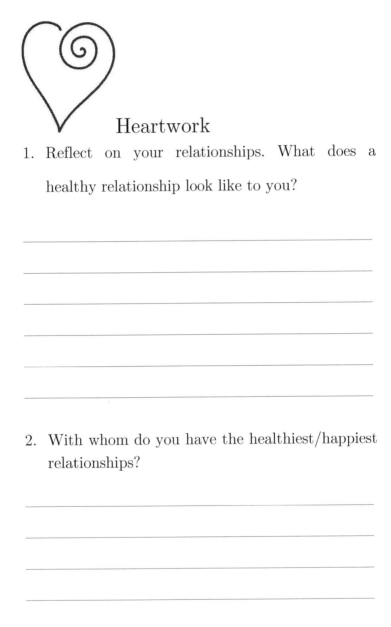

Heartwork

1. Reflect on your relationships. What does a healthy relationship look like to you?

_____

_____

_____

_____

_____

_____

2. With whom do you have the healthiest/happiest relationships?

_____

_____

_____

_____

_____

3. Do you feel better or worse when you are around these individuals?

_____

_____

_____

_____

4. What behaviors do the people you have healthy relationships demonstrate that you most admire?

_____

_____

_____

_____

5. Now reflect on the opposite. What does an unhealthy relationship look like to you?

_____

_____

_____

_____

6. With whom do you have unhealthy relationships?

_____

_____

_____

_____

7. Do you feel better or worse when you are with these individuals?

_____

_____

_____

_____

8. Have you ever shared with them—in a loving way, and only if it is safe for you to do so— what they do or say that makes you feel uncomfortable?

_____

_____

_____

_____

9. Are you ready to let someone know that you will not tolerate an unhealthy behavior?

_____

_____

_____

_____

10. Do you feel like you need professional help in this situation? Do you know who to ask? Do you know who to turn to? If not, ask someone you can trust.

_____

_____

_____

_____

_____

11. On a spiritual level, our challenges are gifts. I have had a series of negative relationships over my forty-plus years on Earth and they were instrumental in me learning how to love and respect myself. A lack of self-love is the basis of a lot of the personal pain we endure. I'm grateful for these lessons because as I learned to

love myself it gave me more love to share with others.

Love for the self and lack of love for the self both can be transferred through generations. No matter which we receive from our families, self-love or self-denigration, it's up to us to decide if we want to change how we feel and treat ourselves or maintain it.

Take a few moments now to reflect: What are some of the beautiful traits that have been passed down to you from your family? (For example: Were your parents, aunts, uncles, and grandparents funny, kind, and driven with big hearts)?

12. How may you emulate these?

_____

_____

_____

_____

_____

_____

_____

13. What are some of the traits your family passed
    down to you that you wish to change because
    they are not beautiful (For example: Did your
    parents, aunts, uncles, and grandparents put
    work before family, have an addiction, such as
    alcoholism; were they anger, or too dramatic)?

_____

_____

_____

_____

_____

_____

_____

14. What are three things you could do right away
to begin to change them?

_____

_____

_____

_____

_____

_____

6 BODIES, SHAME, AND SEX

DO YOU REMEMBER THE FIRST feelings you experienced centered on your body, yours or someone else's? Was it confusing to try to understand what they meant? In my recollection, I was just a little girl. I don't even remember my age. We were in town visiting my grandma and grandpa for a holiday break. I had made friends with another little girl. I can still remember what she looked like although I can't remember how we met. I went to her family's holiday celebration and all the kids were playing hide and seek. We hid together in the backseat of her parents' car and she was lying on top of me and started touching me inappropriately. I was curious, scared, and ashamed. I had never had any feelings like those before about my body. I don't know how much longer it was after that, but I was playing doctor with my cousin, a boy who was close in age to me. I recall that I asked to see his penis because I was curious, but then shame came over me.

Since my mother had me when she was fifteen, it was ingrained in me that the same was not going to happen to me. My mom put me on the pill when I was that same age in fear that I might follow in her footsteps. She likely gave a sigh of relief that she didn't have to worry. For me, this gave me permission to be curious. I had sex with my boyfriend, who was the first boy I ever really liked. Then I found out that he'd had sex with another girl and my heart was broken. I had thought I was the only one. I wasn't. I thought the relationship would last forever. It didn't.

Because of how heartbroken I was about that boyfriend's behavior and the abuse and unreliability of the men I had seen in my childhood home, I decided that men couldn't be trusted. When I started dating new guys after that, if I felt like it was getting too serious or that a boy was losing interest in me, I would break up with him before he had the chance to leave me. I was determined to have the control this time. To say I had major trust issues is an understatement.

Recently I was horrified to learn the statistic that 80 percent of teen boys these days have watched porn. Eighty percent! I am the mom to three sons, and I don't like what porn could do to their minds. When I learned this fact, my fear started increasing. Before then, I'd had no idea I needed to be on top of this or that it is such a big problem in our society. When I was growing up, boys would look at dirty magazines and we just didn't talk about it. Today our young men are learning that the images they see in pornography are the way girls should be. That this is what's normal.

We need to stand up for ourselves and our girls and teach boys and men how to love and treat us right. The men in boys' lives need to set the example of how to treat women appropriately too. Girls should also be having similar conversations with adult women about their sexuality and how to protect themselves from being treated like objects for male pleasure. If we don't talk about it, then how can we change it? Stop being embarrassed by what's happening behind closed doors. Help others be aware and to set expectations and boundaries for themselves.

My beloved biological father whose existence I learned of when I was ten passed away a few years ago. He became my teacher of what unconditional love from a man is supposed to feel like. The men who were in my life before I got to know him did not represent the male gender as honorably as he did. Because of how they treated my mother I felt ashamed of myself. As a teen I decided that if I valued my life in any way, I had better figure out how to make it in the world and provide for myself, and one day, my children. I did not want to rely on a man.

I am sad to say that sex became something I felt I had to do to keep boys interested in me. It wasn't particularly enjoyable. I wasn't a young woman who had embraced her inner goddess and danced for her partner or let herself go completely during lovemaking. I was ashamed of my body. So much so, in fact, that when I was twenty-seven, I got breast implants.

Here's a funny/not-so-funny story about what can happen as a result of not loving your body enough. I had been on a modeling job in South Beach, Miami, with the Stetson Man—a male model who had been hired to pitch their brand of cologne. Although I was happily married by then and not interested in dating this male god, I still wanted him to perceive me as beautiful. I had put fake boobs that looked like chicken patties in the cups of my swimsuit to enhance my shape. For one shot, we were asked to jump in the pool holding hands and then climb out, and as I climbed out the photographer stopped me to point out that my chicken-patty boobs had fallen down into my suit. Everyone looked at me and I felt entirely humiliated. Ashamed.

After having a baby, I had to shop in the training bra section of Walmart because I had inverted nipples from nursing. I didn't want my husband to see them because I felt they were ugly. My husband has always been one of the sweetest men you will ever meet and would never hurt me intentionally. In fact, he always uplifts me. One day I was in the bathroom and had just showered. He asked why I always covered myself and I told him because I was embarrassed. He then wrapped me in his arms and told me he loved me and that I would always beautiful to him no matter what. Even though he was very kind, when I made the decision to have the breast implants, I did it because I didn't like my breasts.

Now more than ever in our selfie world so many girls and women criticize their bodies mercilessly. They can only see imperfection as they look in the mirror. Their eyes go to all that they believe is wrong and they compare their features to perceptions of how they should look that are not even real.

Sister, I'm here to tell you that what makes you beautiful is *not*—and please, please hear me—*what you look like!* You want to talk about *sexy?* Sexy is and will always be kindness. Sexy is humility. Sexy is being confident.

Sexy is not ego. Sexy is not your booty or boob size. Sexy is *love.* Sexy is compassion. Sexing is *respecting yourself and others.* Sexy is patient listening. Sexy is doing something to make the world a better place to live.

Sexy is not the car you drive or the size of your bank account. Sexy is what you do when no one is watching. It's who you are when no one cares.

Sexy is not just existing. Sexy is *living.* Sexy is helping your sister out with a dream that she doesn't know how to navigate on her own. Sexy is boldness and courage.

Sexy cannot be measured by the likes on Facebook or the hearts on Instagram. It's not your number of follow or unfollows. Sexy is a concept that's totally overused and misused by people who have not awakened. It's time to awaken.

Sister, we all were born beautiful. The goddess in each of us should not feel shame or guilt for her curves or the thinness of her frame. So what if a woman has a thin frame? So what if she is round and voluptuous? Why should any woman be shamed for her body? Why should we judge others and ourselves so harshly? I see shaming happening all the time. Women and girls shame other women and girls whether they idolize their bodies or don't. It's ridiculous. Just ridiculous. If you talk meanly about other women, my bet is that you talk meanly to yourself too in the privacy of your own home.

What kind of human being are you? Do you care about enhancing your appearance because you are treating your body like a temple and feel like a goddess? Or are you constantly fussing with your appearance so you can get attention and praise. If you feel amazing and beautiful, isn't that so freaking wonderful?

At first, I have thought my value was based on my body and on winning a title in a beauty pageant. Then I thought my value was based on being the kind of mother or wife people thought I should be. Then I thought it was based off my bank account and my number of friends. I thought it was based on my public image and my growth. For a long time, I measured myself against people who were further along the road of success than me (or so I thought) and this kept me running my engine in full-throttle mode for years and missing out on a lot of the life around me. I was chasing an illusion, thinking it would bring me joy, only to find out that success in this mode made me feel tired and annoyed. The marathon of my workload was exhausting.

My point here is that the idea that anything outside the love we embody is an illusion. Our bodies are gauges that show us if we are healthy or sick. I can look in the mirror and tell immediately if I haven't been treating myself with kindness. We need to correct the messed up thoughts in our heads that make us feel ashamed of our incredible bodies.

Aging

When I was in my teens I really wanted to be in my twenties and when I was in my twenties, I wanted to be in my thirties. Now in my forties, I have no interest in going backward. There is so much life to live and with wisdom comes peace and I feel more peace now in my life than ever before. But I really want to dig into this conversation here because I believe it's more of an issue than we speak about.

Teens into college years. Many teenagers can't get jobs or have no time for jobs as they are so overwhelmed with school, sports, and family obligations. The pressures of drugs and peer pressure are for sure heavier than what I experienced as a teen. This generation is now witnessing families literally not gathering, and if they are gathering, they are gathering on their phones and looking at the screens on their handheld devices. They're lost in a virtual world of never-ending stimulation. The chemicals released in the brain during this behavior is the same chemical released when someone gets a high from a drug. In essence, there is rampant addiction to virtual reality. This generation is being chased by the media. Youth is being revered while aging people are being tossed to the curb.

Many cultures and traditions celebrate aging unlike our western tradition of sending the elderly to nursing homes and hospitals. Aging can be a scary thought for many women because they fear becoming obsolete. A lot of people feel like they lose their value and that they're not important. I've never understood this. I've always craved learning from people who were older and wiser than me, but I think what's interesting is that a lot of people aging stop growing and evolving. Could this be why aging is looked at as a negative in western culture?

There are many countries where elderly people are honored, countries such as Greece, Korea, China, India, Africa, Italy, and Native America. The tradition of honoring our elders is carried down generation after generation. This too can be a bit of a heavy weight though. I believe somewhere in the middle is just beautiful. Everybody ultimately longs for the wisdom of age while maintaining the vitality of youth, as much as possible.

Recently a friend in my town asked when I was ready to embrace my elderhood and when I would stop dying my hair? I had been battling this question for the last five years. Starting around thirty-five, my body began to change, so did my hormones, skin, and hair. I would work out so hard and yet I looked in the mirror and was disappointed. I kept comparing my body to the images I stored in my mind files. You know the images of how good we *used to* look or that image of the girl your age whose body looks like that of a twenty year old.

Every single time I looked in that damned mirror, I would feel like shit, so I stopped looking in the mirror! Yes, I did. I would glance to throw some makeup on, glance to do my hair. But I didn't know *who* she was—this woman I had become. I didn't take care to see her beauty at every decade of life.

I responded back to my friend that I couldn't answer his question. Isn't it interesting? This came from a man. My very own husband has asked me to go "gray." Well, as accepting as my husband is, I actually feel like I am honoring me now more than ever.

I used to roll my eyes at the girl who would talk about her nonstop sexual experiences with her partner and how incredible and magical it was. I was bored and thought something was wrong with me. Oh, and there would be no lights on in the bedroom during sex. *Foreplay, what?* Nope, I heard all these women smiling and fantasizing about their sex lives, and as I listened, I only felt more shame and curiosity. *What is wrong with me?* I wondered So I got the testosterone shot, progesterone shot. Any shot there was to help, I wanted it. The toy shop. *What am I missing? Why can't I be more like them?*

I read every book in the *Fifty Shades of Grey* series, visualizing the "Christian" moments with my husband. I talked my husband into going to see the movie on Valentine's Day and I was mortified when he leaned over and said, "Honey, you really want to do these things?" I said, "NO! NO! Of course, I don't." Which I really didn't.

The movie was not as good as the book. My imagination was much better.

But let's get back to hair. Yes. We're aging, let's just get over it. Stop crying about it. Use the creams, dye your hair, buy makeup, if it makes you feel good! Don't do it because you are trying to hide from yourself or be someone you think the world wants you to be! Dance with every age of yourself!

You have made it this far, sister, and you deserve to do whatever you wish with that hot, beautiful body of yours. Don't be ashamed that you want to still feel beautiful at any age, whatever that looks like and means for you!

Now when I get my hair done it's almost like a ceremonial experience for me. I'm honoring myself and embracing the feminine side of me that I enjoy and which I neglected for so many years. I live in a household of men. Every sport I attend is played by boys. We don't take ourselves too seriously at home, and for sure we don't have emotions flying around the house. Everything is pretty chill at the Dreilings, so much so, in fact, that for years when I went to put on makeup, I *hated* doing it. I mean despised it. Doing my hair was a pain in the ass, and oh don't even get me started on getting my nails and toes done. (I always freak out thinking about how well or poorly sanitized those mail places are.) This was my outlook on living in the feminine mask.

But once again. Why did I deny my femininity so much? Why did I not honor my beauty or femininity? And then it became apparent. I lost her. When I was growing up with three sisters, I did all the things sisters like to do: do makeup, fix hair, play school. I was in beauty pageants. I got attention for being pretty. For being a good little girl in the world. For wearing my crown and showing the world that I was a good person doing good things.

See, I would think, *I'm not "poor white trash."* My constant craving to become an image that the world would accept made me as hungry as a lion staring at a steak. I needed validation. I needed love and connection and I needed to feel important. So I played the role. The role that got the most smiles and received the most head turns.

But a girl can only go so far before she wants to run from it all. Then what happens? I have sons. I force myself to dress down, I pay for the bill at the restaurant, I don't cook, I don't do laundry. Anything I view as remotely feminine takes a back seat for me.

My attitude was: I am now going to embrace my masculinity and I'm not going to drink this cosmopolitan and sit by the pool and talk about people. I wanted to get away from it all.

Even though I was in a female-dominated business, I didn't want any part of the feminine paradigm anymore and that's where my tendency to be one extreme or another brought me out of balance.

Accepting the decade that we are in is so important. Honoring it. Cherishing the next ten years and feeling excited about what will be learned and what will be overcome. I actually feel like I'm getting younger, so the concept of aging to me seems so foreign, although obviously it is a reality. I'm human and have been tested and my ego had to be tamed a bit.

I believe the key to happiness and successful aging is really loving where you are and staying in your own lane. Be inspired by another but don't wish you were them. Don't wish you could go back. Don't wish you could be something you're not. Love who you are right now and love where you are going.

Stop judging a woman because she ages better, or is skinnier, or prettier, or gets better grades, marries a better husband, is richer, kinder, and gets more likes on social networking sites. In the big scheme of things, women comparing yourself to someone else's "better model" is a neverending road to unhappiness and unfulfillment. The constant comparison mode will leave you energetically drained and depleted of joy.

Instead admire the *beauty* in every woman who has more than you (or what you seem to think is more) like a beautiful piece of art work. Honor her beauty. Don't pick it apart and for sure STOP PICKING YOURSELF APART. Just as you honor another woman for her beauty, it's time to honor yourself and your decade. Honor your decade of contribution and growth.

Ask bigger questions of yourself, like: What does the world need more of? The answer for you may come in the form of writers, artist, singers, performers, scientist, teachers, humanitarians, entrepreneurs, mission workers, mommies, grandmas, earth lovers, lovers, animal lovers, friends, speakers, truth speakers, and so on. You get to choose.

Make the next decade interesting. Make it magical. Love the decade you're in. Every strand of gray hair on your head, every low-hanging boob, every saddlebag or wrinkle, every curve . . . love it.

Most importantly, ask yourself, *Am I loving myself and the world the best I can?*

So, what have you learned here? Turn the page and let's do some heartwork now.

Heartwork

1. Do you ever feel ashamed of your body? If so, why?

_____

_____

_____

_____

_____

_____

2. Do you find yourself comparing your body to other women's bodies a lot? If so, why?

_____

_____

_____

_____

_____

_____

3. Do your friends and peers talk about body image in a positive or negative way?

_____

_____

_____

_____

_____

_____

_____

4. Do you find yourself taking pictures of yourself posing sexy to get more likes? If so, why?

_____

_____

_____

_____

_____

_____

_____

_____

5. Do you struggle with a food, alcohol, or drug addiction? If so, have you sought help?

_____

_____

_____

_____

_____

_____

6. Have you ever had a negative sexual experience that made you afraid of expressing your sexuality? If so, have you spoken to someone trustworthy about it?

_____

_____

_____

_____

_____

_____

_____

7. Do you eat food to get fuel or for another reason, such as to "silence" negative feelings?

_____

_____

_____

_____

8. Do you have a generally poor or a generally positive self-image?

_____

_____

_____

_____

_____

9. Do you know how to eat in a way that fuels your body or are you confused by nutrition?

_____

_____

_____

_____

10. Where could you go for instruction on your
    health?

11. Are you willing to commit to providing your
    mind, body, and soul with healthy food, positive
    self-talk, uplifting people, and inspiring
    experiences?

12. If not, what would it take for you to be ready?

If you are struggling with a poor body image, you should know that you can program your mind with affirmations to be more accepting of your body and more self-loving overall. Affirmations are true phrases written in the present tense and beginning with "I am" that reinforce positive attitudes and actions. If you repeat them several times a day, with feeling, like you mean really them, they will become a part of how your mind works.

Try these affirmations or make up some of your own.

- I love my body.
- I am perfectly imperfect.
- When I get off course, I correct myself without shaming myself.
- I spend time with like-minded people who fill their minds and mine with positive intentions.
- I will see the beauty in myself and in others. I am here to learn not to judge.
- There is no failure only learning.
- I accept my sisters for where they are in their journeys.
- I am the light and I shine the light.

- I am responsible for how I am showing up in the world.
- How I show up makes a difference.
- I will reach out my hand to offer love and an ear to those who are willing to change and grow.
- I am in love with positive growth and I am committed to a better me.
- I engage in activities that build me and others up.
- I love my body and I am unafraid of sex. I share sexual experience only with those who honor my body and my soul and respect me for that which I am and that which I am becoming.
- I forgive myself for any past choices I made that were not in alignment with my greatest self.
- I learned the path I don't want to travel and charted a new course for myself.
- I choose to live for today.
- The present is the present.
- The past is behind me and the future is waiting.

- My choices today are a compass for my future.
- I may not yet be where I want to be, but I am on the path to get there.
- Every choice leads me somewhere, so. I choose wisely.

7 The Art of Forgiveness

HER NAME WAS STEPHANIE. The only real best friend I ever had. A great one. One who loved deeply and authentically. And then there was me. The poster child of a girl who overcame great odds and adversity to be one of the few women to be in the top one percent of entrepreneurs, but who was so afraid to have a relationship with girls that I pushed away anyone who got too close before they could hurt me.

I shared that I had this tendency with Stephanie. I told her to not be surprised if I tried to push her away. It was a pattern I was working hard to overcome but had not mastered yet. I told her to not take it personally if I did. I would work through it, I would eventually figure out how to let her love in.

When it happened, I don't even remember why I was trying to push her away. But the day came. She stood there and she put her hands on my arms, looked into my eyes, and said, "Christy Dreiling, I love you so much, you will never push me away from you!" She meant it. She loved me.

Wait, I thought. *This is abnormal. Why would a woman love me? Except my mom and my sisters, they've never loved me before. They only hurt me.* I was thinking of jealous girls in high school who called me names and some betrayals from friends when I was modeling. *I gave them my heart and they crushed me like I was nothing and then they were gone. Like the men of my childhood. One day there, the next day not.*

Boy, it caused me a real internal conflict to try to trust someone. I struggled with human beings in general. *Trust* is a five-letter word for a feeling that creeps into my life every now and then and tests me to see if I'm really awake and paying attention.

This was about a decade ago. My business was collapsing because the economy was collapsing, and my finances and I were in deep shit. But Stephanie was there. I had a large tax lien on my house, my car had been taken away, and the IRS was banging on my door. We had one vehicle left, my husband's.

Stephanie was working as my assistant at the time. She had let go of her nine-to-five job to come work for me. She was incredibly talented. Brilliant and the kindest person you could ever meet. She drove me to a hole-in-the-wall used car dealership in the not-so-good area of town. She knew of my financial struggle. It was embarrassing. I was so ashamed of what had happened, but she didn't judge me. She was by my side.

We sat in this dealership with hubcaps on the wall and the ceiling literally falling down and I looked at this car salesman and said, "Okay, so here is the deal. I need a car for X dollars a month. I don't care what the interest rates are, but my credit is horrible." He looked at me like I had three eyeballs and laughed.

I felt humiliation and shame as we left. Even this man couldn't help me. Stephanie reassured me that I had the strength I needed to get through it.

I remember visualizing my life. *Have I already lived my highlight reel?* I wondered. *Are the best moments of my life over? Will I ever bounce back? Why am I such an idiot? Why did I put myself in this situation? Why didn't I ask more questions?* I wasn't the best with money and in retrospect I take 100 percent responsibility for my mistakes, but I blamed my advisors back then for the choices I made. I was a young woman who had started making more money than I'd ever imagined I'd ever have and no financial training, so I made some wrong decisions.

The entire reason I left "average life" was that I wanted more for my babies. I love being a mom. I had always wanted to be a good mom growing up. I wanted to lead by example and show my kids a better way than scraping out a living. I wanted my kids to look at their mom and say, "Wow, thanks Mom, for showing us how to be a great human who does great things."

Thank God they didn't know what a failure I was in that moment.

Our financial crash was met with desperation. The humiliation was unbearable when we went to my husband Scott's parents asking for help to bail us out of trouble. The lecturing they gave us was like having thousands of needles poking at me. In the end, we chose to work through this crisis on our own.

Basically, I had to set aside my pride and put on my big girl panties and deal with what was really hard. I had messed up. I had made a lot of mistakes and I had to learn from them the hard way. But this was not the end of my story. I determined that I would take my setback and make it a comeback and I would then use it as an example to help others.

Let me put this in some context for you. My team's revenues had dropped from $50 million a year in sales to $20 million. All at the same time, many of the leaders I recruited resigned. I would be lying if I told you that I didn't want to give it all up like them. I even tried to convince myself that life would be easier if I let all the material things go. I could live in a car with my family for a while and not deal with all this crap. I was so close.

But my boys! Their beautiful blue eyes melted me. I looked into their eyes and saw my and Scott's legacy. We couldn't be selfish now. We needed to do something to improve our circumstances for the sake of our family.

Life isn't easy and if anyone tells you it is or acts like it is, they shouldn't be taken too seriously. The real question when life gets tough is, do you fall down and stay down or do you recognize the moment for what it is and create a plan to meet the challenge? You must decide that you are someone who won't give up or give in.

You can decide now without waiting for a crisis. Repeat this phrase until you believe it: "This is only for a moment. I will not only survive I will thrive."

What happened? I bounced back. I decided to throw most of my energy into assisting an incredible woman to build one of the largest sales teams in my company. Sounds like a beautiful ending to a sad situation doesn't it? I could say "The End" right now and you might feel better about your own struggles and possibly inspired to go through the fire knowing that others are waiting for you with a medal saying, "Great work, girl?"

But that's not the end of the story.

A couple of years after the Christy crash, things with Stephanie began to change. We developed different interests and moved in different directions. My husband and I began hanging out with new people. I can't explain why we drifted apart. Scott and I would have arguments over it, and I would say that I just knew I had to move on. A friendship that had once felt so effortless and easy now felt painful and hard. My pulling away caused hurt feelings and led to a full breakup. Ugly words were spoken. The judgment, drama, and pain were so much for me to deal with that I even unfriended Stephanie on Facebook.

On Memorial Day weekend we received a sad call from a mutual friend. All I can remember is that I went into shock at the news. I was numb. I wanted someone to wake me up from a nightmare. There had been a boating accident in which Stephanie was injured. She was being taken by helicopter to a hospital.

What does this mean? Will she recover? What exactly is wrong with her? I thought.

We rushed to the hospital where many friends had gathered. I embraced her mama and papa, whom I love deeply. Her dad cried in my arms. The man who had been driving the boat kept saying, "I'm so sorry. I'm so sorry." I felt like an intruder. But I tucked away my shame to focus on supporting these people whom I truly loved. Regardless of what had been said or done, I loved them. As Stephanie was fighting for her life, I held her children in my arms and heard them begging for their mama not to leave them.

The tears. The pain. The regret. The shame. Unbearable sadness.

Stephanie passed away never knowing my deep true love for her and my gratitude for the difference she had made in my life. Even as I write this, tears fall down my cheeks. My love for her still runs deep. We would finish each other's sentences. We could read one another's minds. We traveled to spiritual retreats together. She was the friend I had always wanted and didn't believe I deserved. The pain of losing her before we could reconcile was terrible.

The silver lining is that I learned an important lesson from the loss: that I need to forgive anyone whom I feel has harmed me as quickly as possible and myself for my mistakes. Life is too short to hold a grudge and to keep the people we want in our lives at a distance.

Learning to forgive others and ourselves is not easy. It takes patience and practice. After Stephanie died, I decided it was time to forgive my father, for leaving me when I was little. For years, we'd had a relationship, though we weren't super close. Even so, occasions of being with my dad were some of my favorite times. When he would visit, he made me laugh so hard I would almost pee myself. No one else made me laugh like him.

Now I had a strong feeling that I needed to take my dad on a private father-daughter getaway first, and then also to treat him and his wife and my mom and her husband to a trip to Guatemala with Scott and me to do mission work.

The father/daughter trip was layered with love, laughter, memories, and stories that only we could appreciate. We had a chance to clear the air. He took the opportunity to read my book *LOL,* in which I describe how I felt growing up poor and all the struggles I went through. He told me of his regret that I'd felt so much pain, and I assured him it was not his to bear. That it was alright because it had made me the woman I am today.

The second trip was also rewarding, but difficult, to say the least. As you can imagine, all kinds of emotions arose from bringing my parents together. These led to a meltdown in which my mom shared all her anger and frustration with my dad and my dad listened and took it all in. My dad said he was sorry. Then my mother accepted his apology.

A few months later, my dad died.

It was December near the holidays. The phone rang. I answered. It was my stepsister, who said, "Christy, dad died. he's gone." My immediate shock turned into me lying on the floor begging for him to come back. But he wasn't coming back. The man I had finally let into my heart and let love me was now gone. Fortunately, the forgiveness we'd experienced left me only with love for him. There were no recriminations like "Should I have reached out more?" I had said "I love you" and he had too.

There are those of us who have a harder time forgiving ourselves than others. We must learn not to carry so much pain from guilt on our shoulders and to be gentle on our developing souls. We must remember that we're all still trying to figure out how to fit together the pieces of the jigsaw puzzle of life. Our mistakes and missteps are one of the universe's ways of humbling us.

If we go off course, forgiveness can help us get back on course. Sometimes forgiveness can take years—and it's okay if you are not ready yet to forgive as long as you have the intention to heal and release your guilt and anger someday. Setting an intention is a good way to start your healing journey.

Others of us hold on tightly to our anger. We must remember that by holding on to feelings like anger we only hurt ourselves in the long run. Emotions are energy, which aligns with matching energy. So if you hold on to anger, other angry people will be drawn to you. As long as you are angry, you may never really feel safe or settled. That's why forgiving them can be one of the kindest things you do for yourself, your family and your future.

Heartwork begins on the next page.

Heartwork

1. Do you need to do some forgiving?

_____

_____

_____

_____

2. Do you blame yourself for something you did in the past? Looking at it now, can you see how you were just doing the best you could and forgive yourself?

_____

_____

_____

_____

_____

_____

_____

3. Do you blame someone else for doing something to you or someone you love in the past? Looking back at it now, can you see how holding on to your anger and pain from this event hurts you more than it hurts them? Could you let go of the pain and forgive now?

_____

_____

_____

_____

_____

_____

_____

_____

_____

8 From Me to We

I FAKED IT. I DID.

No not *that*. This chapter isn't about that, girl! What I faked was who I was and what I liked. I did this so other people would be my friends. I did this because I wanted to belong and be accepted. It was a while before I took my mask off and just said, "Screw it if you don't like me!"

So, here I am: Yes, I read my horoscope, and every now and then I love a great psychic reading. I also love crystals and I love spirituality. Note, I didn't say *religion*. I respect religion, but it's not my thing. It used to be my thing. I earned an online bachelor's degree in metaphysical sciences and I have a paper to prove it. I definitely believe in prayer and I believe in love. I also love drinking some wine and I love eating!

I love to travel with my family. I don't like the cold, but I do love me some beach! I *really* hate wearing high heels, but I love the way they make my butt look and I like being taller.

I really can't stand watching the news and yet I'm always open to watching a heartfelt feature story. Before you start judging me about not being current on the news, you should know that there are plenty of people around me who do fancy it, and we've arranged that if the world is ending, they'll bring me a glass of wine so we can go out in style. Sign me up for conversations around food and wine and this girl is happy.

I don't like heavy metal, explicit rap, or any music where the singer screams and shouts. Get argumentative because I don't see the world like you or because I disagree, and this girl is out. I can't stand politics. I always vote for the person, not the party line.

Have you put down the book yet? I hope not.

I give my leftovers to the homeless even if that means my family and I need to drive all over town to find one. I sometimes take weeks before I put my folded clothes away. I stare at them like *I'm going to win* . . . but I never win that battle. I don't like cooking—I'm too impatient—but I *love* to eat. I have talked about food a lot here, haven't I? Oh, and I'm a vegan. But I don't mind if you're not. Do what pleases you!

I admit, I do sometimes get my feelings hurt when I smile at people and they look right at me and don't smile back. I love yoga. I love meditation. I love hippies—at least the ones who wear deodorant. I have a soft spot for kids and people who are hungry to change. I love books. I have a serious fetish for books.

Now, I could go on and on about *me,* but the point of doing this was to see if anything got stirred you up inside. If you made it this far, then you passed the first test in becoming a *we* sister. If you put the book down, then you'll never know my point. See, we humans have a tendency to push away that which is unfamiliar. That which we do not understand. That which is not like us. Even if your preferences are the opposite of what I shared about mine, I still love and respect you. I don't have to agree with you to love you. I am interested in *you.*

We do draw to us, more often, that which is like us, don't we? But I'm not persuaded we should be complacent about who we spend time with based on superficial differences. I believe there is value in diversity. Switching from a being *me* oriented to *we* oriented means that we pay attention to what we are feeling. Our feelings can teach us a lot.

One thing I wish more women would do is to celebrate and embrace the success of other women. When we celebrate a woman's success, we're giving ourselves permission to be successful. Instead of doing this, however, I have found that if a woman is more accomplished or successful than them either other women will beat themselves up for not being at the same level of accomplishment yet or they will talk negatively of that woman to make themselves feel better. Instead of seeing her brilliance and her beauty and drawing closer to learn more, some women push away.

Why are we really pushing away from another woman? Is it because she is reflecting to us something inside that we know we are capable of? Maybe, we're too afraid still to see this greater self and we don't believe we are worthy of it. Seeing another woman living her dreams can remind us that we aren't yet living our own dreams or reaching our potential.

A while back I did a series of inspirational video messages called "Coffee with Christy." I couldn't believe that people would watch them from all over the world. They would tell me that my chats changed their lives. A few said they even saved their marriages.

What?! I was just ranting on video.

For years I had a feeling that I needed to share my thoughts out loud though I didn't because I thought I needed to make a big production out of it. That I needed to have my hair and makeup done. One day I heard a voice in my head say, *Just do it. Forget the makeup, forget the hair. Just do it.* I was standing in my bathrobe and my hair was in a towel and I did it. I was scared because I was just really putting myself out there. No makeup. Just Christy. Sharing from her heart.

The messages I received in response to that one video were incredible. People were inspired because I was being authentic— "being real." The more I did the videos this way, the more I knew that this was who I naturally am and that I had been trying too hard to fit into a mold that wasn't Christy.

Compliments followed. At first if someone mentioned that my teachings were a lot like Gabrielle Bernstein or another motivational speaker, I would tense up and get irritated. Sure, they meant it as praise, but I didn't want to be like anyone else. Honestly, I didn't even know who Bernstein was back then and when I saw her books at the airport I turned away because I didn't want to be accused of copying her. I was annoyed. Part of me felt upset that I had been teaching these principles for years and had always wanted to put them into a book and that I hadn't believed in myself enough to sit down and write one.

Finally, I stopped being so stubborn and I bought one of the books and I fell so in love with Bernstein's sense of humor and her teachings (yes, many were similar to mine but many were different too) that I bought dozens of books to share with other women as gifts.

Normally I wouldn't get uptight about being introduced to the work of another successful woman; normally I would pull her stuff close to me. But even during the writing of *this* book, I felt some discomfort come up when I was out to dinner with some peers who are beautiful souls with big hearts. I shared my new passion for bringing women together and one woman said, "Oh, like Rachel Hollis?" I said. "No, I don't even know who that is."

After that I almost didn't keep writing this book because I was afraid it would look like I was a copycat. When I shared that response with my daughter-in-law, she said, "You must write this book! Women need this! We need this! Sage [my granddaughter] needs this." I took the advice from my daughter-in law-and got back to work.

This was worthy of examination. I wanted to understand why I was so worried about writing about topics that have been written before. Upon reflection, I realized that just like there are many ways to communicate religious messages, there are many ways to communicate other messages. My style may work for you and it may not. It may connect with your heart and it may not. I may not be smart enough or have enough educational degrees for your taste, but I am certain that I am someone else's cappuccino. Even if this book only gets put in the hands of a few women, I will be so honorably proud to leave my message for my children and grandchildren and generations beyond.

I have been meeting more and more remarkable women everywhere I go. So many brilliant ideas, companies, and noble and admirable work are coming from women that I want to get closer and build a movement around them. I've been connecting women to other women individually for a long time, now I intend to gather female hearts together to do *great shit!* (That may just have to be printed on a tee-shirt: Women Do Great Shit.) My intention from now on is to ensure that all women and girls have access to the resources they need to promote their products, services, and ideas—so they can go far with them.

Recently, I started a podcast where I interview women about their stories. I ask them about their successes, their pains, and their goals. The intention of this podcast is to link like minds. To gather our hearts and experience and turn this crazy ship of a world around. I do not care what your profession is, if you have a plan to change the world, I want to know you, connect with you, and talk to you. You should be a part of *we,* you are a part of *me.*

I know that this may sound Utopian and I really don't care. I don't care how imperfect my plan is or even if you like or dislike me. I care about making this world better. That being said, I know we are better together. The sun does not ask for anything in return. The moon does not either. The rain, the flowers, the trees, the earth. Nature selflessly gives to us and we take, take, take. When we do not give back to the planet, we stop the cycle of life.

The me-oriented aspect of our society today has become pretty heavy. I fought against doing selfies on Instagram for the longest time. I mean, for years. But the more I resisted it, the more I was losing love and connection with people who wanted it with me. If you are a person who loves to serve, like I am, it's not about what you're getting out of it, your question should always be centered around "What can I give in order to serve?" I was disgusted with where the tides of change had led us. I had to change my story about it.

I decided that when I posted selfies it would always be me living my life. Showing people that to live means to love your life. I don't want or need people to tell me how great I am. I want them to know how great they are, how valuable and deserving there are of living beautiful lives. In the process of making this internal adjustment, I learned that part of self-love is self-expression. We can paint stories of our lives on social media that are a form of artwork.

You are a piece of artwork. You are a painting. If you post a picture of yourself somewhere, your post reveals something about your essence and the things for which you stand. As a member of a conscious collective of women, you will be celebrated for being you and you also will celebrate other women for being themselves. We will lift one another up. We will ask, "How can I help?"

If you find yourself wanting to compare yourself to another woman or to judge, give more. It feels amazing.

Have you ever felt not included in the "cool girls" club? I remember being younger and never quite fitting into those groups. In high school, I hung out with everyone from band members to members of the drill team. I didn't want to get stuck in any one classification. I wanted to explore the hearts of all the students. Not much has changed except that I really have no use or tolerance for people who want to complain about life or have a victim mentality.

I'm not interested in gossip or negative talk. But if you want to gather to talk about your dreams, goals, and ways of getting over your hurdles then you can count me in! When you gather with other women, be kind, loving, and an influencer by helping your sisters grow and contribute. We should not be the same in all our groups. We should establish many groups with many types of people, each who challenges our habitual ways of thinking and being.

When you gather, open your heart to other hearts. If a woman you meet does not have the same faith as you, get to know her. Ask her about her faith. Be interested! If a woman works in a profession you know nothing about, ask her about it and why she loves it. If she comes from a different background than yours, ask her about it. If you are too quick to judge you could miss out on a lot that life has to offer. Imagine liking one type of food, one type of art, one type of person. How boring! Only when we gather and explore our diversity can we expand!

The mission of the gathering movement is to connect girls and women to others who want to help them realize a goal or a personal dream. We all have so much to add to the world and often what keeps us from jumpstarting our vision is the lack of support, belief, and or ideas. Let's say you want to write a book and don't know where to begin. Well, a gather sister may be able to lead you in the right direction. Maybe you want to start your own business and you're not sure how to go about that. It could be that you want to homeschool your children, but you're not sure how to start! Sometimes we just need advice on life and could use a little inspiration from someone who has been there and done that before us. The purpose of our community is this.

This would be a dream come true for me. Women igniting each other's minds and hearts. Women supporting one another! Women celebrating in the success of other women!

I got my first taste of the power of women supporting other women through my current business. I remember attending my first meeting and a group of women were celebrating me for doing something I had no idea I had done. They were giving me roses and cheering me on? What? What planet did I land on? At first, I was crazy skeptical. I was waiting for a surprise. But there wasn't one. I was receiving genuine encouragement. Ever since then, I've wanted to extend this culture so the rest of us could experience how great it feels.

Turn the page and do some heartwork.

 Heartwork

1. List all the women in your life that you know
   are reaching for a dream or desire.

_____

_____

_____

_____

_____

_____

_____

_____

_____

_____

_____

_____

2. What can you do to support them? Can you connect them to someone? Buy they product? Give them a referral? Share their company? Give them a compliment?

_____

_____

_____

_____

_____

_____

_____

_____

_____

_____

_____

_____

_____

_____

_____

3.   Is there a woman in your life who has championed you? Have you told her thank you lately?

_____

_____

_____

_____

_____

_____

_____

❧

I imagine a world where we become each other's biggest cheerleaders. I see women daily put themselves out there to share a product that they love or an opportunity they love and the people around them can be just down right mean or nasty. I see family members not supporting them and talking about their "little dreams" as if it was some fantasy or an embarrassment. Some women are not strong enough to prove them otherwise, so their dreams die inside of them. They fall into the trap and they never live their best lives.

Is it crazy to think that we can really change this around? Women supporting women on every level? High-fiving a sister for wanting to better her life and her family's life?

It's not uncommon for me to see a woman who works eighty hours a week as a single mom and she's trying to make ends meet start up a side hustle to earn enough extra money to allow her time to be with her babies more. She bravely shares her product or service with other women and sometimes she is supported or maybe even pitied, but what hurts the most is the women who look down upon her and judge her.

Remember, we don't know people's stories and why they choose certain professional vehicles for themselves. It's important never to judge people. Instead, listen to them, hear what they say about their struggles and their pain. Can you help them? Can you encourage them? Can you redirect your own spending on products to their stores?

We've been conditioned to believe that going to a big box store and buying something off a shelf is "okay." I truly don't think that people really think about supporting small, woman-owned businesses and so we need to bring it to the world attention. We need to highlight women who are working to make their lives better and the world a bit brighter.

9 Kindness Creates a Ripple

IMAGINE A WORLD WHERE YOU could walk into any room full of women and you'd be greeted by smiles, hugs, and handshakes. Imagine your daughter coming home from school and sharing stories of the random acts of kindness that happen to her each and every day or sharing news of the acts of kindness that she had done that day and how good they made her feel. I believe with all my heart that such a world is possible. I do. If you and I can envision a healthier and kinder place for ourselves and our daughters, we can build on that vision together.

When another woman is mean to you or someone you know, do you try to get back at her? Do you give your friend ammo to retaliate? What is your response? How you respond in situations like these is either contributing to the problem of women being petty and mean to each other or helping solve it.

You can be sure that if a woman is being mean, someone has treated her poorly or in a hurtful way in the past. She is expressing or sharing her pain inappropriately, but you do not have to recycle her negative energy. You can make a different choice.

We must remember that hurt people are the ones who hurt people. If we can begin to understand, and I mean *really* understand this, then we can teach our children to react differently when verbal "stones" are being thrown at them. And we can practice responding differently when someone does something spiteful and malicious to us.

We can teach our daughters that they do not have to be mean to survive. That they are stronger as friends. Everyone can learn to use kindness and love. If we demonstrate compassion and kindness to someone who is in pain, it is my view that this might change the trajectory of her entire life. It may be like turning on a light in her dark world.

I am not supporting those who are mean, ugly, and hurtful. I am not suggesting that we allow people to harm us recklessly. But I am suggesting that since we cannot change anyone, since we can only change what we ourselves do and how we ourselves feel inside, then maybe we should start there.

Ways to respond when you are on the receiving end of negativity include:

Communicating. Reach out in a kind way to the sister who you perceive as being mean to you or upset with you and say, "You know, I sense there is something bothering you and I am wondering if everything is okay. Is there anything I can do for you?"

Say: "You know, when you said [whatever she said] to me the other day, it really hurt my feelings and I know that this was likely not your intention, do you have some time to chat about it?

If someone is really angry and mean, it's best just to be kind. Trust your feelings about how to do it. I have gone as far as sending cards anonymously (making sure they didn't know my handwriting) and saying something super kind. Sometimes sending a gift in the mail or leaving a gift for someone with them never knowing where it came from is enough. It can be gratifying to see the changes in a woman after spreading kindness quietly to her.

Sometimes if we try and offer kindness publicly, it will be pushed away or make the people angrier because they are resisting love. People with traumatic pasts often will do this. The kinder you are, the meaner they can get.

Most ideal is to avoid hurtful people, but before you exit, sprinkle a little love around.

When you yourself have hurt someone or even hurt yourself with mean words, you might want to do the following.

Calling yourself out. You know when you have gossiped or been mean. First and foremost, just *stop!* When you feel yourself going there and you begin saying something or doing something that's not in alignment with the kind sister code, stop and self-correct ASAP. Do not blame or shame yourself, just self-correct.

If a friend starts to gossip with you, you could say, "You know I read this book called *Gather* and it really inspired me to stop gossiping or saying hurtful things about others and myself. I am not perfect at it, but I am really trying. I just know that it feels better and makes me happier. Do you mind supporting me?"

Reaching out and asking forgiveness can be a brave and honorable action. It's not easy to call ourselves out when we have messed up and acted out of alignment with our higher selves, but we must practice radical humility.

Frankly, we also have to be detached from outcomes. You may do the right things and say the right things, and some people still just won't like you. For whatever reason, they just have something against you and it's not always rational. I repeat, we must remember that we cannot change others. But we definitely should not change ourselves to meet someone else's standards either. We must be authentic.

Perhaps we can agree that mistakes are lessons.

There has been some really cool research done on what happens to our bodies when we do random acts of kindness! (Visit RandomActsofKindness.org for details.) Researchers have learned that not only do our own brains release endorphins when we act nice or kind, but the people receiving our kindness also get an endorphin release. Endorphins are hormones that heal our bodies. Did you ever wonder why you feel great after running or lifting weights? When we exercise, this chemical releases into our bloodstreams. Endorphins are nature's way to encourage us to get off the couch. They are very important to the well-being of our minds and souls too. If you're in a bad mood, exercising to boost endorphins is a quick way to feel better.

How cool is that?

Let's consider changing the world by being kind. When my friend Stephanie was alive, she and I along with our other friend Callie would take our kids out to do random acts of kindness. One day we would pick up trash on the side of the road, another day we would leave money on top of a vending machine, on Valentine's Day we stood outside with a sign that read "FREE HUGS" (we stole that idea from someone we saw on YouTube) and we also gave out roses that day, too. Oddly enough, about 25 percent of the people didn't want a hug at first because they thought we were asking for money. They asked us how much a hug cost! We reiterated, "FREE," and they were shocked. Most took a hug once they grasped that they *really* didn't have to pay for it. Sometimes we would pay for someone's coffee at the coffee drive-through window or pay someone's toll on the freeway.

Doing random acts of kindness makes us feel good even as it puts a smile on other people's faces. But you must commit to not wanting any recognition for your kindness. Sometimes people are kind for the wrong reasons. They want to feel significant and to persuade other people that they are nice. They hope to get something in return. I suggest you do this for you. Do it because it brings you joy. It's best to let go of expectations.

As I am writing this book I am headed home from a work/play trip to LA. I stayed with my hairdresser whom I believe is one of the best men on the planet! I have to shout out to him because he absolutely knows how to spread kindness and love. Richard makes every woman who sits in his chair feel so incredibly special. It's a five-hour makeover every time I visit him! He has my hands and arms massaged, my jewelry cleaned, my makeup done (complete with eyelashes!) and he does not stop until I look better than I ever imagined! He sometimes works on five women at a time and leaves all of us feeling on top of the world! Check out Richard Michaels Aveda Salon.

Anyway, he has a guest house made for a princess that I stayed in on my trip. After one long day, when I came home, I found he had lit three candles lit, turned down my bed, set out a snack for me, and was playing my favorite movie, *The Greatest Showman,* in the background. I wanted to cry! He totally "gets" it. He is someone who creates a ripple of kindness. His name is Richard Michaels and owns the Aveda Salon in Costa Mesa, for those of you curious about setting up a gather girls' trip!

If more people could just step outside of their problems and fear and settle into gratitude and appreciation for their lives and the people in their lives, then they would see a dramatically different world before them. Nothing is more beautiful than a kind, loving person who genuinely cares and is willing to spread good vibes and love wherever she goes.

Try it out for yourself, do it without expectation and then see how you feel. It may take you by surprise that everything you're searching for you already have access to it. It's in your heart.

Get creative and you can start many ripples of love.

 Heartwork

1. Is there someone that you need to have a conversation with who has been treating you oddly? Do you feel comfortable talking to her? How do you think she will receive it?

_____

_____

_____

_____

_____

_____

2. Are you prepared that she may not receive it in a positive way? Could you detach from the outcome?

3. What random acts of kindness have been done for you?

_____

_____

4. What kindnesses have you done for others?

_____

_____

_____

_____

_____

_____

_____

5. What are some ideas of things you could do for
   yourself, your family, your friends, or strangers
   to spread the love?

_____

_____

_____

_____

_____

_____

_____

_____

_____

6. Who is always doing a great job of showing you love with whom you'd like to reciprocate?

_____

_____

_____

_____

_____

_____

_____

10 Trust Again

WE'VE ALL BEEN HURT—SOMETIMES more than we want to acknowledge. But it's important we admit it to ourselves. I know this kind of admission may be tough, as it can sting to remember what has happened! To me, it says so much about you that you're willing to take a deeper look at yourself. The truth of the matter is that when we put ourselves out there, we sometimes get hurt. We may even "let" people hurt us.

You may insist, "Christy, I don't *let* people hurt me, they just do." But I would remind you, as I often remind myself: Unless you are a child, no one can hurt you without your consent. You have a choice of how to react to other people's actions.

If a malicious person lays hands on me in my home or workplace, I have a choice whether or not to put myself back into the same environment afterward—and I probably wouldn't do it. If someone speaks to me in a harsh or confrontational way, I have a choice of whether or not to let them steal my sunshine, and also of whether or not to retaliate. I don't have an interest anymore in either starting or playing a role in any human dramas.

I've told you that I put borders around my heart to protect myself when I'm around people who've hurt me before. I set boundaries. Some boundaries are healthy. We all should be cautious when we're around those who have a history of hurting or offending us—for example by posting negative comments about us on a social network. Anytime there is such an incident, we have to discern the reason an action like this has taken place. Was it an accident? Is it out of character for this person to behave this way? Did she make amends? Has she tried to make it right? If so, then our trust should not be affected.

Like I tell my kids, each of us has an emotional bank account and we make deposits and withdrawals in one another's accounts. If you constantly make withdrawals from the people you know, you will deplete your accounts and your relationships will begin to suffer. If you catch this happening, you have to be smart enough to get help to stop it, have a conversation, or move on if the relationship no longer serves you or the person involved.

Sometimes if we guard our hearts too fiercely it gets in the way of relationships that we would like to be closer with family members, friends, and colleagues. I have had to work on trust because of my childhood. I spent my entire life guarding my heart— even not entirely trusting my beloved husband, a man who has never betrayed my trust! He was "guilty" only of loving me deeply. But because of my past experiences with my mother's husbands and various boyfriends before I met him, I worried that if I let him love me, he would leave me.

Having had the experience of entrusting friends with my personal information and finding out they shared it with others, I stopped trusting most friends with similar details. I decided it wasn't worth the risk. I'm not saying I am right to do so, I am only reporting. My mistake was trusting too much and then being taken advantage of—and feeling upset.

Many women are exceptional givers and people pleasers. If you are someone many people count on, you could begin to feel resentful about saying yes when you want to say no. Sometimes in an attempt to avoid drama we just acquiesce and become a "yes girl." My intention here is to encourage you to really dig deep and ask yourself if you are missing out on a lot that life has to offer because you either don't trust enough or you trust too much? Looking at your past and present, reflect on these issues without judgment.

Or flip this. Perhaps you know someone who doesn't trust you. Do you understand that this is not necessarily a judgment of your personhood— that is, unless you have given them a reason not to trust you? Please realize that everyone is carrying some baggage from the past.

Patterns of trust and mistrust can be very deeply engrained in us. Take my case, not only did I mistrust my husband, bless his heart, I also had a hard time trusting my children. Most of the time they never gave me any reason not to trust them. I simply wasn't able to trust people. I am the kind of mom who purposefully has her nose in her kids' business—although not to the point it gets weird. I just deeply care and want to stay tuned in.

Everyone makes mistakes, especially while they're growing up. We don't have to fear that our children are going to get in worse trouble than we ourselves did. In my opinion, as a parent you have to decide where you can let slide a little and make their own choices and where they need a little more guidance and involvement from you.

Trust has been one of my most challenging lessons. I'm not there yet, but I'm getting closer. I really am. Life keeps offering us the same lessons until we get it right. In focusing on this issue, it began showing up everywhere until I finally decided I would pass this test.

Someone cheats on us, someone lies to us, someone says or does something incredibly hurtful, or someone steals, betrays, ignores, or forgets us. Someone makes a promise and doesn't keep it. We set expectations for ourselves and those we love and when they aren't met, we can feel disappointed, angry, mistrustful, or afraid. We therefore protect ourselves.

Repeating patterns are interesting. Years ago, I trusted two guys with a large sum of money. Miscommunication occurred. I lost the money. Skip forward several years. I got into a new business deal with two men. I was happy and on top of the world. I just knew this deal would be amazing. Then I found out that the men had misused the funds for our venture. Here is the startling part: I lost the SAME amount of money that I'd lost before.

Evaluating both scenarios side by side, as a pattern, I can see I didn't ask enough questions.

Did history repeat itself because I didn't learn the lesson the first time? Maybe. Coincidence? I don't know. But I can tell you that I now insist on reviewing the small print in contracts and I double check figures in the financial statements I read because if a mistake is made (and mistakes are *often* made) then at least I know that I have done the best I could. Earlier, I didn't have that kind of mentality.

The first time I lost funds, I shamed myself. Really badly. The second time I decided would not fall into a pattern of self-brutalizing. I decided I would learn. I would get better, not bitter.

Part of the lesson was to pay close attention to my thoughts and actions to ensure I was not putting myself down or beating myself up for making a mistake—and also to be certain I was keeping my heart open! I understand that I cannot expect people to trust me if I don't trust them! That said, I also believe that trust is earned. It's important to move slowly to make certain that all parties in a group or business deal share values and have a moral code.

We have to really listen to our hearts on this one. Our instincts too. Sometimes we are going to get it wrong. Really wrong. But that's just a step on the path of getting better.

I am aware that to some of my readers it will seem weird to say that I am grateful for all my "wrongs." But I am, because I learned from them. Through being wrong I have been able to build my character and establish a core set of principles for myself that work to protect my interests and keep me free. This way I can trust myself more.

Let's do some heartwork.

 Heartwork

1. Is there an area in your life where you have lost trust in yourself? What area is that?

_____

_____

_____

_____

_____

2. Do you keep repeating a negative pattern in some area of life? If so, what is it?

_____

_____

_____

_____

_____

3. Have you asked for help to heal a negative pattern? If not, where could you go for help?

_____

_____

_____

_____

_____

_____

4. Is there a person in whom you have lost trust?

   What happened?

   _____

   _____

   _____

   _____

   _____

   _____

   _____

5. Did you move on after losing trust or are you

   actively focusing on the pain?

   _____

   _____

   _____

   _____

   _____

6. Are you holding yourself back because you feel mistrustful? Where and how?

_____

_____

_____

_____

_____

_____

_____

7. Are you avoiding relationships because you are not able to trust?

_____

_____

_____

_____

_____

_____

8. Are you someone who can be trusted?

_____

_____

_____

_____

_____

_____

9. Have you lost someone's trust by sharing something confidential?

_____

_____

_____

_____

_____

_____

_____

11 LET'S START A MOVEMENT

LET'S START A MOVEMENT IN which we take personal accountability for who we choose to be and how we treat one another. This movement must begin with respecting ourselves and respecting our differences. We've talked about so many topics in this book, and even so I know it's only scratched the surface. That's why I hope we can gather locally and help one another by talking about areas of special interest in our own communities.

I believe it's a woman's natural instinct to be loving and kind. Babies are not born angry or mean. When people act out, they are showing us a glimpse of how they feel about their lives. Through compassion and understanding, we can begin to help them heal—in ways we cannot by simply contributing to the judgments they are already putting on themselves and the world.

The Gather Community is a place where we can share our ideas, dreams, hopes, and wishes, and network with one another to help the sisters on our right and on our left achieve their dreams. If you can help another sister because you have a gift to share, then please do! Share the love. We must also celebrate one another growth and achievements, even if that means we don't have a "highlight reel" to show off yet. We must work on being genuinely happy for one another. Through all my years, through tears of disappointment and smiles of joy, I have learned that those who are the happiest are those who are happy for others.

Let go of the burden of trying to be perfect or feeling desperate to get awarded medals and titles. Just be authentic in whatever moment of your life you are in. Be yourself. And be happy for other women when they are being successful being themselves.

There are times that my number one focus is being a mom because that's what I feel I need to do at that moment. There are other moments when I need to focus on my husband, my business, my health, my finances, my friendships, or my creativity. Sometimes I just need to listen to my spirit and be true to my heart, not mold myself into the shape of someone else's dream for me. As I get older, it is easier for me to be my genuine self and appreciate others for being themselves too.

In concluding this book, I only want to say how much I hope that you will choose to join the company of wonderful likeminded women and do great things together. When you gather, it doesn't have to be complicated, fancy, or a big deal. Just come together and find ways to serve each other's best interests and enthusiasms. You know how to do this because you were born with this natural ability. I know that you can light up the world just by being you. But I promise, we are so much better together.

Set a powerful intention to do good and be kind. Then start small and watch your intention spread. As more women like you and me put our ideas into action with support from others, we will see our dream become reality. If we don't follow through with those actions, then we are just dreamers warming up the bench on the sidelines of life.

Most importantly, be kind. Be kind to yourself and everyone you know and meet. Life isn't perfect and we are not ever going to be near perfect, but we can count on kindness being the elixir for our unhappiness. It will warm the spirit and soul on any dreary day. We will be tested. It isn't hard to be kind, but it does take discipline to be kind to everyone consistently. So, let us make this a practice, knowing that nothing good ever comes from being unkind.

When one individual suffers, no one wins. Yet suffering has become too normal in our society. Rather than being addicted to suffering and unkindness, we must begin to be addicted to compassion, kindness, our dreams, our people, and our lives. Go with the flow of your life and be ready to take on everything that comes with grace and radical humility.

Be the rain in the fire. Be the calm in the storm. Be the sun in the dark and be the wind for the sail. Be the teacher for the student and be the student for the teacher.

Be the strength for the weak. Be the faith where there is fear. Be the love where there is hate. Be the difference in the same.

Be the spark for the dream or be the grace in the grief. Be real where there is fakeness. Be the vision where there is no sight and be the dreamer who takes flight.

Be yourself, the beautiful you. You are like no one else. Unique, bold, beautiful, smart, fearless, courageous, fun, flavorful, colorful, interesting, creative, sensual, sexy, wild, free, freaky, goofy, rare, ordinary, extraordinary, sweet, feisty, committed, persistent, dedicated, passionate, and confident. Careful or careless, glamorous or frumpy.

We are just beautiful, aren't we? I mean absolutely, stunningly beautiful.

You are one of a kind and you are designed to be that way. Your song to sing is *you*. Your life is waiting for you, as life is waiting for us all.

Why are we waiting? Why have we waited so long? We must shine. We must grow. We must travel. We must explore. We must ask questions and we must forget, yet never be forgotten. All of our beautiful colors, shapes, and sizes matter. Real women. Real girls. Real life. No longer settling for illusions of a fake world, we are honoring ourselves and the divine feminine power that exists in each of us. And we can honor the divine masculine that lives in us too.

We can be fabulously fearless badass boss babes who are radically kind and humble. We can. Being all these things and more begins with one single step.

It begins with you and me coming together.

Let's gather.

Acknowledgments

I AM SO GRATEFUL FOR MY husband, my three sons, my daughter-in-law, and my grandbaby, who all encouraged me to go to the coffee shop and write and then sat patiently as I would read a chapter to them and get excited. They excitedly demanded that I finish this project. My husband held me accountable to getting this book written even in moments when I started doubting that I had something to say.

I thank all the women who have come as teachers and students into my life. The women who have been begging for the release of this book so that they can gather with others. Becky Vaughn, who really helped me get the vision of the cover on paper for me to see. Editor Susan Strecker, who worked on my first drafts, and the one and only Stephanie Gunning, who subsequently took my fears of editing and laid them to rest, helping me create a book that is now a manifestation of my dreams.

I humbly acknowledge my higher power, my God, my spirit guides, my master teachers, my angels. Especially you, Dad, Steph, and Grandpa. I know somehow you have had something to do with all of this. You were always my biggest fans and you always taught me unconditional love. May the work you do on the other side and the work I do down here change millions of lives and make the world a bit better of a place. I love you.

RESOURCES

Visit my website: christydreiling.com
Email me at gathermovement@yahoo.com
Follow me on Instagram: @gathermovement and @christydreilingbeauty
Friend me on Facebook: Facebook.com/Gather Movement and Facebook.com/Christy Dreiling

ABOUT THE AUTHOR

Christy Dreiling is a loving wife, mother, grandmother, leader, and humanitarian. In her previous pursuits, she was a fashion photographer, model, actress, Miss Kansas Teen USA, and Mrs. Kansas United States. She rose to being one of her company's top income earners by successfully branching out into many markets and world cultures.

Christy is the author of four books. She produced an award-winning documentary and is working on another film based off her third book, *LOL*. She's started a company called Prosperity Panties that hasn't succeeded, and basically now has thousands of panties in her storage unit. She also started another company called A Million Dreams Entertainment that didn't go anywhere. She has yet to finish her master's degree in metaphysics, an educational goal she has been working on for the last seven years. Bottomline, she is still working hard to learn how to save and not give money away, and even though she has succeeded a great deal in life and business she has also failed a great deal too. She is particularly proud to have an awesome family and works hard to set a great example for her babies and grands. She's moved to a pretty cool hippie town in Southern Oregon and has never been hippier (or happier).

Made in the USA
Columbia, SC
04 May 2019